Marriage Stands, Commitment Wins

Published Books by FAAD Publishing LLC

Where's Baby, Momma?

Mello's Dream

Tymzup: Tick Tock

Moments of Gratitude for Black Women: A Faith-Based Journal

I've Passed...Now What Do I Do?

Marriage Stands, Commitment Wins

Vol 1:
Building a Strong Foundation

Sean & Antoinette McDonald

Introducing

Thomas & Zohnette Sligh
Andrew & Desiree Lee
Derrick & Thelma Williams
Philip & Justine Dix
Jermaine & Brittani Williams

FAAD
FOREVER AND A DAY PUBLISHING, LLC

To the extent that the image or images on the cover of this book depict a person or persons, such person or persons are merely models, and are not intended to portray any character or characters featured in the book.

The co-authors and publisher of this book have used their best efforts to prepare this material. Every attempt has been made to verify information and experiences provided in this book, neither the co-authors or publisher assume any responsibility for any errors, inaccuracies, or omissions. .

Published by Forever and a Day Publishing, LLC.
Triangle, Virginia 22172

Special book excerpts or customized printings can also be created to fit specific needs. For details, write to the office of the FAAD Sales Manager: faadpublishing@gmail.com

ISBN Paperback 979-8-9911703-1-4
ISBN eBook 979-8-9911703-4-5

10 9 8 7 6 5 4 3 2 1

Printed in the United States of America

CONTENTS

INTRODUCTION

Marriage is a journey of love, commitment, and resilience. It is a partnership built on faith, trust, and the daily decision to choose each other—through joy and hardship, triumphs and trials. *Marriage Stands, Commitment Wins* is an anthology series that brings together the voices of couples who have weathered the storms, embraced the beauty of companionship, and strengthened their union through life's ever-changing seasons.

This five-volume series is dedicated to exploring the many facets of a lasting marriage. Each book delves into key elements of a strong relationship, offering real stories, practical wisdom, and heartfelt reflections from couples who have lived through it. The first volume, *Building a Strong Foundation*, focuses on the essential principles that sustain a marriage—from faith and trust to shared values and unwavering support.

Throughout this series, you'll hear from couples who have navigated challenges together, learned the art of communication and conflict resolution, kept love alive through life's demands, supported each other's personal and spiritual growth, and discovered timeless lessons to pass on to others. Whether you are newlyweds, seasoned partners, or preparing for marriage, these pages offer guidance, encouragement, and the reassurance that love, when nurtured, endures.

Marriage is not about perfection; it is about perseverance. It is about standing together when the world shakes and choosing commitment when emotions waver. We invite you to turn these pages with an open heart, to reflect on your own journey, and to find inspiration in the stories of those who have proven that *Marriage Stands, Commitment Wins.*

Sean & Antoinette McDonald

Co-Owners

FOREVER AND A DAY PUBLISHING LLC

Sean and Antoinette are the co-owners of Forever and a Day Publishing LLC providing services of self-publishing, financial literacy, proper protection, and educational coaching. The tenets of their businesses; God - Family - Career - Finances are woven throughout all business interactions and transactions.

Sean serves as a central office human resources administrator in the second largest school division in Northern Virginia. He is a career-long public educator with more than twenty-eight years of experience teaching 5 - 12 grade English language arts, reading, math, and adult education.

Antoinette is a retired elementary school principal and has over twenty-two years of experience in the education field as a teacher and building administrator. She is the CEO of the publishing company and is ready to serve as the Project Manager on your literary project.

Sean and Antoinette are spoken word poets; Tymzup and Conscious Sista. They perform on topics of consciousness, relationships, politics, and love. Sean & Antoinette are originally from Pittsburgh, Pennsylvania and have been in Virginia since 2001. They have been married since October 14, 2000 and are the parents of Seani, Nia, and Sean II.

https://faadpublishingllc.com
Facebook and Instagram: @FAADLLC

You. Me. We.

by Sean and Antoinette McDonald

The key principles that have helped us build a strong foundation in our marriage are God, Family, Career, and Finances. God has been central to our lives since we were children, whether we understood it then as a principle that would shape us. God has been our greatest champion in getting us connected and keeping us committed.

From a very young boy, I was raised in the African Methodist Episcopal (AME) denomination and served in my church on Sundays throughout my youth even becoming an acolyte. My faith in Jesus Christ through Christianity was seeded by my mother.

> "I remember being reminded to hurry to get ready on Sunday mornings before the Park Place A.M.E. Church van arrived to pick us up in Cove Place en route to Homestead."

The ideals of being members of a church and serving in our church community was a natural part of any family unit I could imagine even at a young age. God, faith, believing in heaven and hell were non-negotiables.

I recount, "In my dating days, it was normal for me to pray over my date's and my meals, or demonstrate my faith in attending church services or other organized worship experiences as part of the "interviewing" processes".

When I met Antoinette, one of our first conversations involved our respective faith and where we viewed faith as a priority in our own lives. It didn't matter to me that Antoinette was raised as a Jehovah's Witness. I understood the name Jehovah as the name of the same God I served and He commissioned all believers to witness the gospel of Jesus Christ so she was already justified and sanctified, as far as I was concerned.

When we were in college and my choices and decisions were not of God, His Holy Spirit convicted me and pricked my spirit. Having God in my life has allowed me to receive His grace and mercy, over and over again. When I found Antoinette, after she met me, God approved me to make her my wife. This is significant because God led me and physically directed my steps in order to "...findeth a good thing."

"I know my relationship with God has been central to me growing up in what some would call a "dysfunctional" family and community. God has led me to avoid the judicial system. He has helped me hurdle the hood tales of gangs, guns, drugs, and death. God spoke to me and showed me His plans for my life, including graduating high school, attending Clarion University of PA, finding Antoinette, taking her as my wife in 2000, and being committed to being the best husband ever.

Even leading up to me asking Antoinette to marry me, God convicted my spirit to "clean around my own front door" and prepare a home for Antoinette. His quiet still voice told me to stop the fornication and to be honest about who I was, and whose I was. This counsel led me to begin breaking strongholds of womanizing and being a dog and a player. I trusted God enough to tell Him I was committed to Antoinette and that I would please Him in my engagement and soon to become marriage. He emboldened me to tell people, "I am engaged to Antoinette" even though we weren't quite engaged yet. He allowed me to speak it into existence with assuredness I had never experienced before.

I had experienced God's truest presence in my life in my thirteenth year. My pubescent adolescence was absolutely tumultuous. I experienced a psychotic break from reality which led me to be hospitalized for more than five months in a psychiatric hospital. This was a result of God's plan to break a generational curse of a broken-family, an absent husband, a single-parent household, a physically and emotionally-abusive home, and freedom from narcotic and alcohol abuse. One night, while laying in a bed in Children's Hospital of Pittsburgh, my roommate in the bed next to mine began talking with me. In my mental state I did not believe this was reality. However, I went along with the conversation and asked him, "Where are we?" In true kid fashion, he thought I was joking about not knowing where we were. He obliged my curiosity and said, "It begins with "H" and ends in "L". My only immediate thought projected loudly out of my mouth, "HELL?!" He laughed and responded in a loud whisper, "No! We're in the hospital!" Feeling relieved is an understatement to express my momentary lucidness.

I still didn't know why I was in the hospital. I didn't know why he was in the hospital either. God "woke" me up that night! He showed me that He was still protecting me from any tricks of the enemy who tried to steal my right-mind! He showed me that hell, hospital, and "heal" all begin with "H" and end with "L". I agreed to let God begin to "heal" my mind and my heart. He brought me a mighty long way from my time in Children's Hospital and afterward St. Francis Psychiatric Hospital. God revealed to me that He has a much better plan for my life, and His testimony through me will be a "witness" of His faithfulness to those who believe. I've been seeing and experiencing God's permanent foundation in my life since then. My marriage with Antoinette is another example of His million little miracles with which He has blessed me.

I (Antoinette) was raised as a Jehovah's Witness and while an adolescent attending the Kingdom Hall through the week and on Sundays, it provided a foundation of belief, focus, and servitude. Watchtower and Awake magazines were studied nightly and provided instruction on serving Jehovah, respecting others, obedience, the commandments, discipleship, and other topics focused on being a witness for Jehovah. The structure of the religion provides comfort and a monotony that is routine and safe for any child. Being at the Hall with my mom, father, and brother always was a treat and built a confidence in a marriage desired for my future. Seeing my father lead prayer in our home as my mom became subservient in leading over us was invigorating. I knew then, I wanted to be married to a husband who leads us in God's Word with fervor and in faith. Years later I found out that my dad was not a Jehovah's Witness and attended the Hall with us because he wanted what I desired too...a structured home obedient to God. Around the age of 8 my father became absent and my heart cried for the structure and consistency that was only present when he was leading. The worldly views, spirits, ideology, and evils are strong and when succumbed to those, my dad chose those ills over our family. Over time, my mom began to lead prayer with a towel draped on her head. This custom only happened when a husband was absent. Through her eyes' sadness I would mumble my own prayer:

Dear Jehovah, Please provide me with a peace and love that will be Yours. Make me a wife and mother who loves You. I need You to keep me protected. Amen.

My mother continued, for a few months, to maintain our prayer and study life but I believe the weight of managing a home, kids, and work became a lot to carry. We transitioned into a new flow, a new reality. My father chose alcohol, drugs, and a new woman while my mom chose me, my brother, and her life! Throughout this abrupt and aggressive reality, my personal prayer life never ended, always asking for the same things; happiness, peace for my mom, love, structure, and protection.

In 1996 when I met Sean, at Clarion University of Pennsylvania, he was my mentor. We would meet at Carlson Library to study and oftentimes we would discuss issues of the heart and spirit. He shared his upbringing and I would reciprocate. When I initially told him about growing up in the Jehovah's Witness faith, he asked me if I ever knocked on people's doors early in the morning. He gently joked about how his whole house would go quiet, no movement, to show that no one was home when JWs would knock. I know everyone thinks negatively about us going door-to-door but how else would we share the ministry. What an amazing way of evangelism!! But 'yes' I went door-to-door and I loved it when I was able to share about Jehovah and why we should be more like Him and the importance of being saved.

Over the years, we would have a meal together and Sean always prayed over us, before we ate. I was intrigued by this gesture. I prayed to myself but never aloud. He was always so bold and so sure of himself. He encapsulated a level of masculinity and leadership when he would lead us. It moved into him praying over me whenever I was having difficulty in school or when I was expecting good news. I pictured a future with Sean very early on, he was indeed my mentor but I wanted more. After a while, we were definitely "in the world" partaking in evening sinful acts but Sean 'covered me' in the Lord, as well. My heart knew he was who I've always prayed for and I was thankful for the blessing.

I recall this one particular evening and I flipped to the back of my notebook and caught myself writing notes to our future children's teachers.

Dear Ms. Williams,
Please excuse Sean Jr. from school on Monday. We had family dental appointments and he was not feeling well to return. Please send home any homework and I will make sure he completes it. Thank you,
Mrs. McDonald

Dear Ms. Linton,
Please excuse Se-Andrea from school next Friday. We are taking a family trip and are leaving on Thursday evening. If you can send home any work, she will return it on Tuesday morning. Have a great day!
Mrs. Sean McDonald

These memories crack me up, as it was a foreshadow of being the wife of this man of mine. I admired my mother and the position she attempted to adhere to for her marriage to work. In those years, I saw my father struggle to fit the shoes of manhood, fatherhood, and husbandhood. An overabundance of loss surrounded me as I no longer had the protection of my father. Even through the relationships I had, I knew I wanted to be loved and cared for, respected and protected. One thing that resonated was that I was going to have Jehovah as the head of our household. I knew that His peace was the unmatched key to a successful marriage.

A strong foundation in God gave me the confidence that I was going to be a wife and a mother. I was going to have the opportunity to be the first and only woman to be Mrs. McDonald. I was going to be the mother of Sean's children and his alone. The Holy Spirit was always with me and spoke ever so softly to me about who would be my husband. When I met Sean it was confirmed that I was to be his helpmeet, for life. Trusting in Jehovah's word as I was to be a Proverbs 31 woman no matter the brokenness I witnessed as a child, this is my foundational truth.

We ensured our marriage started on the right foot by making the non-negotiable of 'divorce is not an option.' When Sean formally proposed to me in the fall of 1999 we set our marriage date for October 13, 2001, around the same month we exchanged "I love you" some 5 years earlier. We promised to do marital counseling when we confirmed a venue for the wedding. At the beginning of the next year we conceived our first child, Seani, on February 14, 2000. Her conception was a miraculous one, we could write an entire chapter on this miraculous experience. Once the pregnancy was confirmed we immediately agreed to move up our wedding to October 14th of that year to ensure that she was born in wedlock. Lincoln Avenue Church of God (LACoG) is where we met in September of 1996 for a community service project so we considered this as our place to be unified.

No one forced us to get married or to complete marriage counseling. God showed both Antoinette and me that He brought us together at LACoG, and He appointed us to be married at LACoG. Neither of us were members of the church! Antoinette and I took the initiative, ordained by God, to seek out Pastor Richardson and humbly request to be married there. His only requirement for us to be married at LACoG was for us to complete pre-marital counseling. "Say-less!" That was too easy.

For eight weeks we drove down from Clarion, Pennsylvania to Pittsburgh, PA on Fridays to have marital counseling with Rev. Mark Richardson at LACoG on Saturday mornings. We loved making this weekly trip knowing we were literally headed in the right direction and preparing to experience our own, real-life fairytale. Our conversations going to LACoG were hype with anticipation and reflection from the week lived in between each meeting. We didn't have marriage models our age! Antoinette's paternal grandparents were married for over 50 years by the time we got together but couldn't lean on closer generations of aunts, uncles, or cousins to be mentored through this new journey.

From the first session or lesson, we both were "all-in". We stuck tightly to Pastor Mark Richardson like spinal cords and car seats...we were connected. We shared openly with excitement all the reasons we wanted to be married, including we were already pregnant. We were already aware that getting married before having a baby would dispel the stereotype of "baby mama" and "baby daddy". We were in love and being coached, consulted, and counseled through this process was another demonstration that we believed God's Word and what He teaches about the covenant of marriage. We knew we didn't know anything about what a successful marriage looked like with anyone in our generation or in our parents' experiences. We were committed to learning how to be married and stay married. The goal was to be an example for our future children to learn and grow. It's amazing how determined one gets when you want something better for your children.

We are able to keep God as the center of our marriage by staying in covenant with each other and whole-heartedly believing in the vows we shared and promises we made to each other during our engagement and beyond our wedding day. The Bible teaches us in Proverbs 9:10,

10"The fear of the Lord is the beginning of wisdom."

We were "wise" beyond our years. We have a healthy fear of our Saviour Jesus Christ. We want to please Him and reap all the blessings He has in store for us.

It is easy to say the vows while you're decked-out in the finest linens, in Ghanaian- cotton. It is another thing to live the vows as they're imprinted on your hearts. We chose to live our vows and promises we made to God. Standing Room Only. That's how many people were present to see our union. The people in attendance though were witnesses but we will call them "spectators". Some of them were prayer-warriors who prayed for a sustainable God-centered marriage, while some were trolls betting on our demise. Either way, we knew "With God all things are possible."

So it is, we were married in October, 2000 in front of over 200 family and friends. That evening, sitting across from each other at Eat N' Park we committed to staying true to our vows and always respecting the vows we said in front of God. That next month our first child, Seani (see-on-ee) was born and Antoinette graduated that December. During this whirlwind of life's changes, we remained steadfast keeping God as our center. The one we leaned on for all decisions.

In July of 2001 we relocated to be teachers in the second largest school division in northern Virginia. Leaving Pennsylvania and stepping into the unknown in Virginia with just $32 to our name and an eight-month old baby wasn't a part of any grand plan but we were determined to not return home. Usually when you move to a new housing development, you must provide a deposit and back rent. When the rental office was contacted, they heard our testimony and the office manager only asked for our 'early hire contracts' and our signature to pay the $835 monthly rent for our two bedroom, two bathroom apartment. This is unheard of but we didn't question it. We signed and returned the contract and sent our promissory documents from the school division. Look at God.

On our moving day, as memory serves us, our parents were not there to wish us off or to pray over us..wow, we never thought about this until writing this chapter. Our Uncle Ronnie and brothers Norman and Homer drove with us through the multiple states. There was this sense of accomplishment but ultimate trust that resonated as we traveled and set our minds forward to all that was in store for us. We were so determined to pour our whole selves into our marriage. No option of failure or of returning to the chaos and dysfunction...we were committed to making this work. This was a test of faith.. Our little family of three. In a new marriage, as new parents, in a new state, in a career, in this world as adults interdependently working under the headship of our sovereign Father.

With no steady income, until September 2001, we worked 23 hours a day with Sundays off. Sean worked 15-hour shifts at WalMart (11 p.m. - 7 a.m.) and Babies R' Us (7:30 a.m. - 2:30 p.m.) and I worked an 8 hour shift at Walmart (3 p.m. - 11 p.m.). We saw each other during the baby exchange in the parking lot. A smooch, prayer, and a fleeting goodbye filled our days for seven weeks. We had a cousin nearby but only each other to lean on, the days ahead felt daunting. But amidst the uncertainty, we knew one thing: God had brought us here, and He wouldn't leave us.

You know what? We had some trying times! There were moments when fear crept in, whispering, "What if this doesn't work?" We would look at Seani, so innocent and unaware of the storms we were weathering and we would feel the weight of our responsibilities. Even in these moments of doubt and worry, there was a steady quiet assurance. Each prayer we whispered reminded us that our foundation wasn't built on money or circumstances - it was faith. Faith in God!

The turning point came one evening when, after another long day of work, we sat down to pray in our apartment. We didn't ask for abundance; we asked for provision. God revealed himself that it was time to "upgrade" our living and to trust in Him to make this happen. Within a few weeks we were signing the housing agreement for a new apartment with top-tier amenities closer to our jobs and a better childcare facility for Seani. That moment reminded us that God's provision doesn't always come in grand gestures—it comes in just enough to remind you He's still in control. As in Philippians 4:19 we were learning on God's supply:

> 19"And my God will meet all your needs according to the riches of His glory in Christ Jesus."

From that point on, we made it a priority to pray together every morning, thanking God for what we had and asking for guidance. Now, why would God leave us?

Matthew 6:26 shares a reminder of how God loves His children;

> "Look at the birds of the air; they do not sow or reap or store away in barns, and yet your heavenly Father feeds them. Are you not much more

valuable than you?" We leaned on each other like never before. Each small victory felt like a divine reminder that we weren't walking this path alone.

Looking back, that season of our lives was less about struggle and more about surrender. It taught us that a strong foundation in marriage isn't built on what you have but on who you trust. By keeping God at the center, we found strength, unity, and resilience in the face of uncertainty. To anyone facing their own '$32 moment,' remember this: with faith, even the smallest step forward can lead to a breakthrough.

Are you on the brink of a marital breakthrough? Has your marital foundation been shaken due to moments of infidelity, alcohol, drugs, lies, uncertainty, fear, and doubt? Does your marriage pattern Jesus Christ's relationship with the church?

We encourage you to carve out some time and learn about what the Bible teaches on marriage. You can start by reading Ephesians 5, the entire chapter, and have transparent conversations about biblical marital foundation and how it looks in your marriage. In marriage, husbands and wives become one flesh and this mutual submission (to be covered in a later volume); is this present in your union? Lean into one another and listen. Build or rebuild your marriage foundation.

We challenge you to say this prayer, as you reflect on your marriage:

Heavenly Father,

Please prepare our hearts to learn about and live out Your intentions for our marriage. We want to align with your design created for marriage. Holy Spirit, show us where we have strayed, from Your design, and provide

Thomas & Zohnette Sligh

Pastors

TREASURES OF THE HEART WORSHIP CENTER

Pastors Thomas & Zohnette Sligh currently reside in Frederick, Maryland. They have been married since July 1999 and have been together since 1991. They have three children, Jazlyn, Thomas III, and Zhane who are currently in college and pursuing their individual career paths and dreams.

They are currently the Pastors of *Treasures of the Heart Worship Center (TWC)*, a ministry they began in 2016 and is located in Frederick, Maryland. In the year 2000, they founded *Treasures of the Heart Music Ministry.* The purpose of the ministry is to bring forth the God-given gifts in the lives of others. They have produced several major musical releases and created an award-winning internet/cable TV show (*Treasures TV*). They have enjoyed producing concerts and community outreach events for the past 30 years. Everything done has and will continue to be for the Glory of our Lord Jesus Christ!

www.TreasuresWC.com
www.Thomasslighmusic.com
https://www.instagram.com/thomasslighmusic
https://www.instagram.com/perfectinmyhandscrochet

Building Your Spiritual House

by Thomas and Zohnette Sligh

Every marriage must be built on a strong foundation, especially if it's going to last and weather the unpredictable "storms" of life. This is basic, common sense, wouldn't you agree? Who would want to begin any relationship with a shaky foundation? When a relationship starts off unstable, and nothing comes along to stabilize it, it's likely to eventually fall apart. The truth is, we often don't even realize when a relationship starts off with a "shaky" foundation. No one truly knows the intentions of the person they are entering a relationship with. It's not until a disagreement arises that we discover whether we've made the "right investment." In those moments, we see how the other person reacts to conflict and get a glimpse of their character. This is when we learn whether the relationship can grow and learn from conflict, or if it might not unfold the way we hoped. If both individuals can authentically work through things, then the relationship will have something solid to build upon.

When people are attracted to each other and begin dating—or "courting," as our grandparents would say—it's a huge step of faith. These individuals are seeking to connect spiritually, emotionally, and let's be honest, physically as well. The person may look attractive to them, and they are immediately drawn in! From the very moment they set eyes on each other, a new "foundation" begins to take shape. Let's be honest, most of the time, people aren't thinking about creating a strong foundation when a relationship starts. However, as time goes on and they get to know each other better, thoughts begin to form about what a future together might look like. This evolving perspective starts to build the foundation on which the relationship is built.

On a more personal note, it's important to recognize that we all come with an ancestral background. These are "foundations" set by our parents and grandparents. Whether these foundations were positive or negative, we carry some of that into our relationship. Many problems and conflicts in a new marriage can stem from bad advice and negative traits passed down from previous generations. On the other hand, positive ancestral foundations can provide great guidance and influence in a marriage. As we reflect on our own journey, we can recall instances where family and friends gave us "negative" advice. If we had listened to them, we may never have met or stayed together. We can both testify that when we invited God into our hearts and started seeking His word in the Bible, we discovered that it was the "perfect blueprint" for building a strong foundation. The word of God guides you in starting your relationship in a way that can lead to a "Godly" marriage. We've learned that having an authentic relationship with Jesus Christ, both individually and together, is key to building a solid foundation. The answers and insight are right there in the Bible, straight from Jesus Himself.

Matthew 6:24-27 offers guidance on how to build a strong foundation and how to put it into practice. It's important to build your *spiritual house* on the rock that is Jesus.

> 24 "Therefore everyone who hears these words of
> mine and puts them into practice is like a wise man
> who built his house on the rock. 25 The rain came
> down, the streams rose, and the winds blew and
> beat against that house; yet it did not fall, because
> it had its foundation on the rock. 26 But everyone
> who hears these words of mine and does not put
> them into practice is like a foolish man who built
> his house on sand. 27 The rain came down, the
> streams rose, and the winds blew and beat against
> that house, and it fell with a great crash."

We want to take you on a spiritual journey with us through our experiences. We've found that trusting God as the foundation of our lives has helped us stay strong in our marriage. We're going to share some tips and advice backed by the word of God, hoping to encourage and inspire you in your own relationship. Along the way, we'll ask you some questions. We invite you to share your responses with each other and have a "heart-to-heart" discussion. The goal is to start seeing, through spiritual eyes, what your *spiritual house* looks like. This house you've built together exists in your hearts, shaped by all the experiences you've had together. You both hold the keys to your *spiritual house.* If you've never talked about this before, we hope this can be a starting point for allowing the Lord to guide you into it. He wants to show you that your *spiritual house* is built upon His love. He will shelter you from the storms of life that try to break it apart.

Now, let us formally introduce ourselves. We're so eager and excited to share with you that we got ahead of ourselves earlier! My name is Tom, and my wife's name is Zohnette. We're sitting together on our couch as I write this. She's here sending her warm wishes to you. I type faster than she does, so she asked me to handle the writing while we share our thoughts. I've learned to just say, "Yes, honey!" She does a great job keeping me focused and on task. She has this special look she gives me when I'm rambling, and I've learned to listen. It's made our foundation stronger as we've grown older. After all these years together, she still keeps me on point, and I admit it! I get excited when I talk about God—whether I'm preaching, singing, or sharing how He's worked in our lives—so please forgive me in advance. She's looking at me now, so let's keep moving.

Over the years, our *spiritual house* has been shaky at times, needing many repairs. There were moments when the foundation seemed cracked to the core, and we wondered if it could survive. But we've learned that the Lord is the only one who could rescue us and restore our spiritual foundation. He brought many mentors and loving people into our lives, who acted as anointed repair specialists. In those seasons, they spoke life and victory into our marriage. We also learned the importance of continuing to submit to God's will, so we could change and grow together. Our love and faith in Jesus Christ have given us countless testimonies of His power. He's put us back together more times than we can count, and that's reflected in our *spiritual house.*

Jeremiah 18:2-4:

> 2 "Arise and go down to the potter's house, and there I will cause you to hear My words."
>
> 3 Then I went down to the potter's house, and there he was, making something at the wheel.
>
> 4 And the vessel that he made of clay was marred in the hand of the potter; so he made it again into

> another vessel, as it seemed good to the potter to make."

There have been many times when our *spiritual house* needed to be repaired and reshaped by the Lord's hand. The potter's house symbolizes God's intervention, as we couldn't fix everything on our own. There will be times in your relationship when you won't know what to do or where to turn. But as you learn to trust in the Lord, He will guide and restore your marriage. It's vital to put God first as a couple, and He will lead you back to a strong foundation. Praying together is a powerful way to invite God's guidance into your relationship. A strong foundation is built upon your relationship with God, and the Bible serves as your spiritual owner's manual. We encourage you to make the word of God your spiritual owner's manual for your *spiritual house*. It's the only way to maintain it.

As we share different phases of our marriage and how the Lord has shaped our *spiritual house*, keep in mind that our *spiritual house* is always being built and reshaped. Over 30+ years of life together, our *spiritual house* has gone through many levels, rooms, and landscapes. Just like our physical home has changed and needed maintenance, our *spiritual house* has undergone the same process. There have been rooms we had to clear out and negative influences we had to eliminate. We're not perfect, and we've learned from our mistakes. We've made sure never to let those negative elements back into our *spiritual house* because they hindered our marriage. One constant, however, is that we choose to make God the "Landlord" and owner of our *spiritual house*. He's the one who opens doors and makes a way. With the Bible as our builder's manual, we've learned to follow God's instructions. As we share some of our life experiences, we hope they inspire you to take an honest inventory of the condition of your own *spiritual house.* We're confident that you'll see similarities between our journey and your own.

Now, come join us for a quick tour of our *spiritual house.* Feel free to relax and leave your spiritual shoes on. We don't have much time to share today, but we'll definitely continue this journey with you in the future. Some rooms may be messy as we're still renovating, and there are some intimate areas we can't show, like our bedroom—that's just for us. It's a place of special worship, as God intended for married couples. In your marriage, strive to keep that space sacred, and if you keep intimacy between you and your spouse, God will bless you. Glory to God! As the Bible states in Hebrews 13:4:

> 4"Marriage is honorable among all, and the bed undefiled; but fornicators and adulterers God will judge."

As we walk out to greet you in our spiritual driveway, let us first show you the special landscaping and courtyard around our spiritual home. It is very important to us. The grass you see now wasn't always this green and full of flowers. It used to be filled with rocks and weeds, and we didn't know how to maintain it properly. It took time for the flowers to grow, and we still have to take care of it, keeping it spiritually watered and pruning the weeds. This is done by remembering that the Lord we serve is the "Living Water" who keeps on refreshing us (John 7:38).

Sometimes, negative people and the evils of the world try to take root and discourage what God has entrusted us with. When we gave in to some of that, that's when the spiritual landscape didn't look its best, but we thank God for keeping us planted by

His living water (Psalms 1). If we were to show you the very roots, which are hidden deep under the ground of the flowers, they would represent the time when we were first introduced to each other through a "Divine Seed" that was planted. Beneath that is the spiritual soil and landscaping that came from our parents and grandparents. One blessing we received was having praying parents and grandparents.

Both of our parents loved the Lord and spent their lives serving their church and community. We come from a strong foundation of pastors, deacons, deaconesses, singers, and musicians. Our parents and grandparents truly went the extra mile to bless others in their generation. They were all called by God in their unique ways, and this forms the depth of the soil and the very DNA of who we are, both physically and spiritually. They were not perfect and needed some weeding and pruning themselves, but they always honored God in everything they did, and they never wavered. We want to ask you: What does the spiritual landscape of your *spiritual house* look like currently? When did you have weeds and rocks all around? Do you have green grass and flowers now? What does it look like deep in the soil of your spirit? Take some time to reflect on this with each other. Sometimes, you must allow God to break up the fallow ground and replant your spiritual landscape that leads up to your *spiritual house*. Hosea 10:12 (NIV):

> 12"Sow righteousness for yourselves, reap the fruit of unfailing love, and break up your unplowed ground, for it is time to seek the Lord, until He comes and showers His righteousness on you."

Simply put, the Lord gives you strength to break up the negativity from your past as you both seek Him. This opens the door to unfailing love, allowing Him to shower His living water upon you and your partner, keeping things beautiful in your spiritual courtyard.

Now, let's go up on our spiritual porch. We have something special to show you. We have some light fixtures that keep shining brightly and never go out. We want to show you just a few of them and tell you what they represent. Most of the things outside of our *spiritual house*, in the courtyard and on the spiritual porch, represent times in our lives before we were married. The brightness of all the lights you see spiritually represents something deep. God is light, and these lights shine brightly for us, always.

The light over here represents when we first met in 1991. A mutual friend, who knew I didn't have a date to prom, showed me a picture of Zohnette. I was struck with a feeling I couldn't describe—my heart melted. I knew something was special about her, and that light has never gone out. We went to the prom together, and the rest is history. We would like for you both to think about the first time you met. Remember the spark, the light of love, and the feelings you had in your hearts. That light, which shone bright for us, should also shine brightly on your "spiritual porch." Never let that initial light of love go out in your spiritual home.

Let's walk over to this other light fixture on the other side of our porch. This one represents when we both went off to college and left home. Zohnette smiles as she recalls the tears we shed on that day, not knowing what the future held. She went to Penn State University, and I went to Clarion University in Western PA. I purposely chose not to attend the same school, knowing I wouldn't be able to resist being around her all the time. When we dropped her off at Penn State, I hugged her tightly, and we all cried like babies. You would have thought it was a funeral. This was a significant time for us, as we were growing up spiritually and leaving our parents' homes. As the years went on, I found myself driving through crazy PA ice storms to be there for her. This was a time when we were maturing together in love, understanding the foundation God was building for us. This is when we knew, without a doubt, that God had a purpose for us. Think about times in your union when you've grown and matured together. What lessons has your love taught you?

One more light fixture I want to share with you shines brightly. One night, I attended a service at my campus where a traveling music ministry spoke. A young lady shared her testimony of a life-changing experience and talked about how she met her husband and how they formed a traveling ministry. Later that night, after returning to my apartment, Zohnette called me. She said she had something to tell me. She expressed concerns that if I didn't want to stay with her anymore, she understood. I was shocked, wondering what she meant. Then, she shared the same testimony I had just heard, and after feeling shocked and empty, I realized the depth of love I had for her. I told her I would never leave, and that we were both called to ministry together. That moment was a glimpse of the plan God had for us. It was also a calling for us to marry. Your spiritual light on the porch can represent something similar for you as well.

Jeremiah 29:11 says:

> 11"For I know the plans I have for you," declares the Lord, "plans to prosper you and not to harm you, plans to give you a hope and a future."

When you invite the Lord into the heart of your relationship, you will discover the shared purpose He has for both of you, including a godly marriage. Has the Lord shown you both a glimpse of His plan for your future? Is God calling you to step out in faith in some way? Take some time to talk about your passions together.

Now, come inside our spiritual home. You may notice the shiny doorbell with our wedding rings hanging on it. We make sure it's always ringing and that whoever enters our spiritual home knows that we are bonded together, symbolizing God's love. We keep our wedding rings shining and ringing with God's love. It's important to remember the significance of your wedding rings. They are a symbol before God that should never be broken. The moment you enter through this door represents the very moment we said "I do" before the Lord. Our wedding day was unforgettable, with over 400 family and friends in attendance. As you step through the door, you might be surprised at what you find. Right after we said "I do," we struggled, because we didn't know each other as well as we thought. We placed unfair expectations on each other—she wanted me to be like her dad, and I wanted her to be like my mother. Neither of those things happened, and we didn't know how to communicate through it. We didn't know how to deal with the shock of not getting along, but the Lord, our *spiritual house* landlord, reminded us to open the blueprint—the Bible—and find direction. We did, and He sent seasoned married couples to offer us guidance. The mess you see at the entrance is a reminder of how the Lord taught us to navigate marriage and how He sees a godly union. It's important to remember how the Lord has brought you through, and that's part of our testimony as a married couple.

On the first step going upstairs, this is where we prayed together for the first time as a married couple. We knelt and asked the Lord to make our house a safe haven and a spiritual refuge for our family and others. Right after that, He gave us a biblical mission and theme, which still guides us today. He gave us the scripture Matthew 12:35:

> 35"A good man out of the good treasure of his heart brings forth good things, and an evil man out of the evil treasure brings forth evil things."

The Lord showed us that we were called to bring good things from our hearts toward each other and others. In your marriage, it's important to seek to help others in the way God shows you. A giving marriage opens your hearts to each other and brings joy in encouraging others. This was the foundation for our traveling musical ministry, *Treasures of the Heart*, which lasted 17 years before we started our church. People would come into our home, and we saw poetry, dance, music, and other forms of art from all ages and cultures. We understood it was our mission to bless others. Let's head down into the basement, where this ministry took place. That's why the basement is still physically unfinished. We focused on helping souls and glorifying God, and this carried over to our spiritual home. It wasn't easy, and we had to learn to balance marriage, work, and ministry, but the Lord taught us so much in the process. In what ways are you learning about each other in your marriage? Are you working on a business, ministry, or something else together?

Yes, we have three grown children now. If you head upstairs, you'll see their rooms and how they've matured over the years in our spiritual home. We have twins—a boy and a girl—who are now 20 years old and we have a 24-year-old daughter. We had to learn how to discipline and relate to them over the years. We never discussed having children, but two years after we married, we had our first child. We came from different backgrounds and had different ideas about discipline, which was a challenge. God had to teach us how to approach it. The one thing we learned is that we had to show them love and encouragement at all costs. We did our best to present a united front when it came to discipline, and we followed God's lead. Being a parent isn't always easy, but it's rewarding. From the start, we dedicated them to God and continue to pray for them every day.

Time is flying by, and we have so much more to share with you. Before you go, take a look at the ceiling. You'll see a bright, shining cross. That cross represents Jesus Christ and the importance of constantly running to Him in repentance. It reminds us that He has given us His Spirit to keep going and never give up on each other. That's what keeps our marriage strong. We aren't perfect, but the cross constantly reminds us that God is with us every step of the way, and He's with you too. We look forward to your next visit to our spiritual home. There's so much more to share!

Whether your relationship began on solid ground or shaky soil, it's important to recognize that you can level the playing field with Jesus Christ. Building a relationship with Jesus Christ within your partnership provides guidance and strength to help you persevere. If you're currently dating, remember that you are laying the foundation for your future. You're shaping what your spiritual courtyard and porch will look like as you prepare for marriage. We strongly encourage every courting couple to seek godly premarital counseling. This can help foster better communication and understanding, setting the stage for a strong spiritual foundation. By doing so, you'll be better equipped with spiritual keys to enter your spiritual home when the time comes to say "I do" before our Lord Jesus Christ.

We invite you to attend the church we pastor, **Treasures of the Heart Worship Center**, located in the heart of Frederick, Maryland—just 40 minutes west of both Washington, D.C., and Baltimore. You'll find us at **629 N. Market Street, Frederick, Maryland 27102**, nestled in the beautiful downtown area. We are a fun, loving, and diverse church filled with authentic people. We are a welcoming, creative, and vibrant place to experience God's love. Our motto is, **"Real People, Serving a Real God,"** and we live by it. Every Sunday is a unique experience, guided by the Holy Spirit—not a script. Worship, praise, and flowing in God's Word are at the heart of our services. To learn more about our church, visit **www.TreasuresWC.com**.

We also invite you to explore our award-winning music ministry, **Treasures of the Heart Music Ministry**, and to view our award-winning Internet/cable access TV show, **Treasures of the Heart TV**. Feel free to search for *Treasures of the Heart Worship Center, Thomas Sligh, The Sligh Family, Treasures TV* or *Treasures of the Heart Music Ministry* on your favorite streaming platforms or YouTube to explore our work.

You can also visit **www.ThomasSlighMusic.com** to listen to our music and we pray it will bless and encourage you.

We're also excited to announce that we'll be releasing our first book in the near future! This book will build on the great conversation we've just shared, offering a deeper look into *spiritual house.*

We truly hope to meet you in person one day for a time of wonderful fellowship. Until then, may God continue to reveal the blueprint for your own *spiritual house*, filled with treasures yet to be discovered. The world is waiting to experience the treasures that lie within the very depths of your heart.

Andrew and Desiree Lee

Entrepreneurs

RELY LOCAL JAX and BODYE CELEBRATIONS

Andrew and Desiree are an ordained husband and wife team who were unified in marriage in September 2012. Join them for inspiring events, couple accountability, and a thriving community!

Andrew Lee is a man of faith, integrity, and unstoppable ambition. Andrew is currently retired after many years as a business owner. He exudes leadership as a serial entrepreneur with a heart for service, he is passionate about helping others succeed. Andrew was the owner of *Andrew Lee Real Estate* and *Executive Style Menswear.* He continues to influence, impact, and expose with the very successful *Executive Cigars LLC* which spans Pittsburgh, Pennsylvania and Jacksonville, Florida. Andrew, also was a successful sales professional. His latest venture is dedicated to empowering small businesses through strategic marketing, equipping them with the tools they need to grow and thrive. Beyond business, he is a gifted teacher, mentor, and counselor, always ready to offer wisdom and guidance. His faith is the foundation of everything he does, leading with honesty and purpose. Andrew is an incredible husband, father, leader, and difference-maker seeking to touch lives every day.

Desiree S. Lee is a passionate, friendly, and God-fearing Master Pilates Teacher Trainer for *Balanced Body Education* and has a heart devoted to serving others. She believes that true wellness begins from within and is dedicated to helping clients strengthen their bodies, refresh their minds, and restore their spirits. As the wonder of Bodye Celebration C.O., she brings her gift for teaching with warmth and encouragement to every session, ensuring clients feel supported and empowered. Her ability to demonstrate precise movements while offering clear guidance allows her to connect deeply with those she trains. Desiree is a natural born leader and her resume of influence and purpose are as follows; a principal dancer for Kankouran West African Dance Company, a lead dance instructor of a liturgical dance ministry at her home church in Pittsburgh,

Pennsylvania, an administrator for Gateway to the Arts, project manager for the Oakland, California film company, *Forward Ever Media LLC*, and the assistant director for the Kelly Strayhorn Theater. Faith-driven and motivated, she sees her work as a calling—to uplift, inspire, and transform lives through health and wellness.

www.bodyecelebration.com
https://instagram.com/bodyecelebrationllc
https://www.linkedin.com/in/desireeslee

Producing the Fruit of the Spirit

by Andrew and Desiree Lee

Genesis 2:21 – 24

> 21 "And the Lord God caused a deep sleep to fall on
> Adam, and he slept; and He took one of his ribs,
> and closed up the flesh in its place. 22 Then the rib
> which the Lord God had taken from man He made
> into a woman, and He brought her to the man. 23
> And Adam said:
>
> > "This is now bone of my bones
> > And flesh of my flesh;
> > She shall be called [b]Woman,
> > Because she was taken out of [c]Man."
>
> 24 Therefore a man shall leave his father and
> mother and be[d] joined to his wife, and they shall
> become one flesh."

Growing up in a large Christian family household, my parents wanted us to become members of a baptist church, get a good paying job, and be married. It was also important that each of us obtain salvation and build a personal relationship with God.

I was blessed. I lived in a house where my mother and father were married for thirty-seven years until my father's passing. I grew up watching my father love my mother, work a blue collar job, and serve as a Deacon in our local church. My father was strict, yet he loved us. Occasionally my mother worked part time, but mostly stayed at home. She taught us the bible and how to pray every day before school and every night before going to bed. I didn't realize that living in this home would jumpstart what I believed, as a young lady, for marriage.

From 1995 – 2001, I was in a six-year relationship that I thought would eventually move to being married. There were two very fundamental beliefs that kept this from happening. The first being our difference in our faith. I was growing and developing my relationship with Jesus and He was developing a more science based understanding of faith. Second, our philosophy of roles in the house and work outside the home were not aligned.

I always kept a journal and not long after that relationship ended, I wrote a prayer to God, requesting what I wanted in a mate. I knew that I had to prepare, be in position, and present myself in order to receive my husband. I also wrote a prayer request to God concerning my desire for a husband. This was not a long list of items and needs but I simply asked God to send me a mate that loved and honored Him with all of his heart, and who would love me enough to see God working in me. Six years later, I met Andrew M. Lee and by that next year we were married!

This to me is important when we talk about key principles to building a strong foundation in marriage. Having a deep rooted and personal relationship with Jesus was pivotal to me. My upbringing paid a big part in having an understanding of God, but getting prepared was solely up to me.

Andrew saw me and he saw that I was an image bearer, a King's kid, and truly loved God. He identified with Jesus that was in me. I saw him and understood he knew how to lead by God's example and also loved God with his whole heart. I, too, identified with Jesus in Him. He nor I could be with someone who was "new" or a "babe" in Christ. We had to be with someone who had the maturity, knowledge, and understanding on walking this life with Christ.

Our marriage is rooted in the word of God. We stand by it! We live by it! And even when we fail, we repent and return to it. We are constantly working to be seen as one flesh. Although Andrew and I enjoyed a lot of the same things, it was the ability to lean on each other's strengths that keeps us connected. He creates the vision and I execute the plan.

Lastly, marriage counseling was important. We had twelve weeks of counseling which gave us the tools to course correct when the load got heavy. And we had seasons in which we needed those tools in order to pray effectively. What I have learned in over twelve years of marriage is just as much as I am God's daughter, Andrew is God's son.

If you're a man who's looking for a woman to marry, please consider that a true woman of God is a whole different thing than you've ever heard of. I finally understand why the Bible says that, "when a man finds a wife, he finds a good thing." The scripture makes the assumption that we men understand that it's talking about a woman who is committed to God. Because the same Bible says, "it is better to live on the corner of the rooftop than in a house with an angry woman."

There is obviously a distinction between the two women mentioned, one who is a reward to a man, and one that should be avoided at any cost. Most of us have found a woman somewhere in between these two types. In many cases, our choices as men have led to horror stories concerning wives. The wife who looks to God as her source is a whole different thing. A wife who doesn't just love God but understands the purpose God gave her in marriage is yet another thing. A wife who is steeped in the wisdom of God is something to behold and I know from experience that this is the wife the Bible calls,"a good thing to find". This is the type of wife that is called a "helper" in the Bible. This woman is a type of Holy Spirit to her husband and her household. She is that Proverbs 31:10-31 woman:

> 10 "A wife of noble character who can find? She is
> worth far more than rubies. 11 Her husband has full
> confidence in her and lacks nothing of value. 12 She
> brings him good, not harm, all the days of her life.
> 13 She selects wool and flax and works with eager
> hands. 14 She is like the merchant ships, bringing
> her food from afar. 15 She gets up while it is still
> night; she provides food for her family and portions for her female servants. 16 She considers a
> field and buys it; out of her earnings she plants a
> vineyard. 17 She sets about her work vigorously; her
> arms are strong for her tasks. 18 She sees that her
> trading is profitable, and her lamp does not go out
> at night. 19 In her hand she holds the distaff and
> grasps the spindle with her fingers. 20 She opens
> her arms to the poor and extends her hands to
> the needy. 21 When it snows, she has no fear for her

> household; for all of them are clothed in scarlet. 22
> She makes coverings for her bed; she is clothed in
> fine linen and purple. 23 Her husband is respected
> at the city gate, where he takes his seat among the
> elders of the land. 24 She makes linen garments and
> sells them, and supplies the merchants with sashes.
> 25 She is clothed with strength and dignity; she can
> laugh at the days to come. 26 She speaks with wis-
> dom, and faithful instruction is on her tongue. 27
> She watches over the affairs of her household and
> does not eat the bread of idleness. 28 Her children
> arise and call her blessed; her husband also, and he
> praises her: 29 "Many women do noble things, but
> you surpass them all." 30 Charm is deceptive, and
> beauty is fleeting; but a woman who fears the Lord
> is to be praised. 31 Honor her for all that her hands
> have done, and let her works bring her praise at
> the city gate."

Now compare that woman to the horror stories you've heard, and you should understand why the Bible says, "when a man finds a wife, he finds a good thing". Imagine being concerned with ruling over this kind of woman. Imagine doing anything but learning more ways to love her and to thank God that he allowed you to find her. I know what this is like because I have found this type of woman and I'm in awe of her. She is worthy of honor and respect. The fact that she calls me her leader is humbling to me. With this backdrop in mind, I want to look back at God's original intention as it pertains to marriage and the role of the woman and the man. My desire is to honor God with my life and my marriage represents a large portion of my life. Each day of marriage is an opportunity to please God with how I treat his daughter. I don't always get it right, in fact I'm probably wrong a lot, but I do produce some fruit. I desire to produce 100 percent, that is my goal. In reality, I'm not there yet, but I press towards the mark of the high calling, keeping my eyes on Jesus, while being open to his correction. In doing so.

In order to understand the institution of marriage, I needed to know what God, who was the creator of marriage, intended it to be. However, I also needed to know the role of Man versus Woman, and the correlation with the term 'human' as it is described in the Bible. I discovered that Man (Human) was first created and then formed. Genesis 1:26 says,

> 26"Then God said, Let us make man in our image, in our likeness, and let them rule over the fish of the sea and the birds of the air, over the livestock, over all the creatures that move along the ground."

From the above text we can clearly see that man is referred to as a plural being just as God is plural, he said, "let Them rule", that cannot be overlooked. Since many will not see this as indication that man was created plural, there is need for more evidence and the Bible gives just that in the very next verse. Genesis 1:27-28 reads,

> 27 "So, God created man in his own image, in the image of God he created him male and female."
> 28 God blessed them and said to them, be fruitful and increase in number, fill the earth and subdue it. Rule over the fish of the sea and the birds of the air and over every living creature that moves on the ground."

It is important to point out a few things in light of the previous verses. First, the term 'man' was spiritual creation and not physical being. Second, man was both, male and female, just like God. Third, man didn't mean 'an' or 'woman' as we know it today, this was a spiritual creation as the physical formation had not occurred yet. The text clearly and repeatedly states that man was plural and that he was able to understand the spiritual command that was given by God to be fruitful and multiply. It's equally clear that it was not the original intent for a man (physical) to rule over his wife (man), they were both given the mantle of rulership over the earth. This is critical in understanding the role of wife and husband that we will later discuss.

Genesis 2:5 states:

> 5"there was no man to work the fields." In this verse, it's important to note that this latest term used for man is talking about physical man, not the spiritual man that was referenced earlier.

Genesis 2:7,

> 7"The Lord God formed the man from the dust of the ground and breathed into his nostrils the breath of life, and the man became a living soul."

Here we have a unique situation, because what was breathed into the man's nostrils was the very spirit of man that God had created spiritually which was both male and female, not man and woman. Scholars believe that it took Adam (Man/male & female) around 600 years to name all the animals. It was only after that point that God caused him to fall into a deep sleep and removed his rib and built a woman from it. Notice, Eve wasn't created from the dust of the ground as was Adam, and furthermore, God didn't breathe into her nostrils the breath of life because she already had life in her. I know that this may be hard to digest for some however, it's in the Bible and I think it pokes a huge hole in some of our theology. While Adam was alone physically on the earth the spiritual female (not woman) was part and parcel of himself (spiritually).

We know that spiritually, the female spirit, could hear God and understand everything he said. We know this because the man that was both male and female that was created before Adam was formed, heard God tell them to be "fruitful and multiply" and to rule over the earth. In Genesis 1:15, God commanded the man who still had his female spiritual self living on the inside,

> 15"You are free to eat from any tree in the garden, but you must not eat from the tree of the knowledge of good and evil, for when you eat of it you will surely die."

This suggests that the one we would later come to know as Eve, heard clearly the same command that the Man, Adam did, albeit, she heard it with spiritual ears and Adam physical one's. God concluded that it was not good for man (physically) to be alone in the physical as he was surely not spiritually alone, because he had God with him and he was still a plural being spiritually. Thus, in Genesis 1:18 God said,

> 18"I will make a helper suitable for him."

The term helper means "power" not "servant." Jesus would later refer to going to the father and the father would send a "helper", also.

Eve's very formation speaks to the fact that she was him and in him from the beginning. Adam even says in Genesis 2:23-24,

> [23]"This is now bone of my bones and flesh of my flesh, she shall be called Woman, for she was taken out of Man." [24] For this reason a man will leave his father and mother and be united to his wife, and they will become one flesh."

This is now the basis for marriage and she is not the man's lessor, rather she *IS* him. Yes, the fall happens and she is made subject to her husband and he is given rulership over her as her punishment. However, that was a result of the curse and in Christ, the curse has been reversed.

God never intended Eve to be the man's foot stool but she was made so for the purpose of the curse. Now we have been set free from the curse and should embrace her as she was meant to be, a helper (power) for her husband. I know that many of the readers may have a hard time with these things but think about it for a moment. Those who are so preoccupied with the headship of the man in this world and what it will mean in the eternal world to come.

A woman won't be your wife in heaven and she certainly won't be your servant. I'd like for you to ponder on the verses of John 17:20-26, when Jesus prays for all believers.

> [20] "My prayer is not for them alone. I pray also for those who will believe in me through their message, [21] that all of them may be one, Father, just as you are in me and I am in you. May they also be in us so that the world may believe that you have sent me. [22] I have given them the glory that you gave

> me, that they may be one as we are one— 23 I in
> them and you in me—so that they may be brought
> to complete unity. Then the world will know that
> you sent me and have loved them even as you have
> loved me. 24 "Father, I want those you have given
> me to be with me where I am, and to see my glory,
> the glory you have given me because you loved
> me before the creation of the world. 25 "Righteous
> Father, though the world does not know you, I
> know you, and they know that you have sent me.
> 26 I have made you known to them, and will continue to make you known in order that the love
> you have for me may be in them and that I myself
> may be in them."

From this, we can see that the most important thing to Jesus concerning us was all believers being brought into a oneness with each other and the Godhead. What better place of unity and being one can be expressed except in the place of marriage where we are called to become one flesh? What I've come to understand is that if she is equally yoked with me; she is a power, a helper, a spiritual guide, a true friend, a lover of my soul, a mother for my seed, a counselor when I'm confused, a protector when needed, and yes - a provider. The relationship with an equally yoked wife is like a type of Holy Spirit. I know that Jesus wants all of his followers to feed his sheep and the only way to feed his sheep is to produce fruit for the weary soul.

The fruit of the spirit is only produced through the trying of your faith. You and I have heard of those that claim to be filled with the Holy Ghost, but they have zero fruit to prove it. We all have sin, so I'm not being judgemental, I'm simply pointing out that the testing of our faith will show us exactly what, if any, fruit we have. Galatians 5:22-23 list those fruits as love, joy, peace, patience, kindness, goodness, faithfulness, gentleness, and self-control. Now, in case you think that you perfectly have all of these in the bag, take a look at how the Bible describes what love is.

In 1 Corinthians 13:4-7:

> 4"Love is patient, love is kind. It does not envy, it does not boast, it is not proud. 5 It does not dishonor others, it is not self-seeking, it is not easily angered, it keeps no record of wrongs. 6 Love does not delight in evil but rejoices with the truth. 7 It always protects, always trusts, always hopes, always perseveres."

Notice that leadership and rule isn't anywhere on the list of fruit of the Spirit or in the definition of love. What we do see, is that the moment after Jesus himself was baptized, He was led into the wilderness to be tested. The more I grew in my faith and with church doctrine, the more I understood that I didn't have enough fruit in my life. Sure, I had some, but I was lacking big time. What I did have was church doctrine. I knew the scriptures back and forward. I knew the role of the man in a marriage was to rule over his wife. I knew all sorts of things but I was woefully lacking in the things that really mattered to God.

He is concerned about feeding His sheep, not our rulership over our wife. He asked the apostle Peter three times, "Peter, do you love me?" Peter became irritated, but the message was clear, if you love me, then, feed My sheep. There's no way to feed His sheep without producing fruit of the Spirit. Jesus said that my Father desires that you produce more fruit. Being the head of your household doesn't mean much unless you're leading with the fruit of the Spirit. Some men I know don't rule with the fruit of the Spirit, they rule according to the norms of this world. The fruit of the Spirit doesn't pertain to a gender, all believers must seek to produce Spiritual fruit for His sheep. Imagine a woman having a problem following a man who regularly produced the fruit of the Spirit.

Now, imagine a man having a problem leading and dying for a wife who produced the fruit of the Spirit. If husbands and wives would focus on producing the fruit of the Spirit for each other, leadership and submission would take care of itself. In fact, I think if this were the case in more marriages, we wouldn't have any real problems at all with our spouses, or our fathers and mothers. If husbands and wives aren't producing the fruit of the Spirit for one another, the results can be harmful to the relationship. As a man I may find myself clinging to that old adage, that *I'm the man and you have to submit to me, whether I'm right or wrong.*

In the same way some women, instead of focusing on producing spiritual fruit, they simply become bitter and angry. I choose to believe that God gave you, your spouse, so that your faith may be tested daily and you would learn to produce Spiritual fruit each day as a result; some 30, some 60 and some 100 percent. The difference in production of Spiritual fruit signifies the growth process during our marriage. I choose to think of it that way when my wife does or says something that challenges my patience. I see it as a chance to produce fruit for her and for the kingdom. Just imagine that if you can't produce fruit for your spouse who you swore to Love for the rest of your life, how in the world are you going to produce fruit for those of his sheep that you don't even know? Therefore, you're quite useless for the Kingdom of God.

The Bible says that if the branches in the vine do not produce fruit, the father will remove them from the vine and cast them into the fire. Also, for those who do produce some fruit, the Father prunes them so that they may produce more. Now, with that as a backdrop, if you're still hell bent on dwelling on your role as leader and her submission, I think you've missed the whole point of the Gospel. Yes, we still live in a fallen world and to that end, the man is still the head of the wife according to the curse. However, as a man who has been given so much grace and mercy by my Lord and Savior, I have no interest in holding my wife, whom I adore, to the curse.

Yes, I'm the leader in my home, but my only focus in that regard is how much love I can lead with. I have zero interest in asserting my position over her or my children. My wife and children provide me with the most precious gift that a man of God could ever have, and that is, a real chance to produce the fruit of the Spirit.

If I have any rule, I lay it aside willingly, just as the Lord Jesus laid aside his deity for me. In Philippians 2:5 it says,

> 5 " Let this mind be in you that was also in Christ Jesus, who thought it not robbery to be counted equal with God, but seeing himself as a man, he humbled himself, even unto the shameful death on the cross."

If the Lord wasn't concerned with His lofty title but was willing to lay it down for me and you, who am I to lord over my wife and children, with my title as leader, or ruler. If by some miracle my wife honors me as her leader, I accept that and I'm truly humbled by it.

Remember, that the Bible tells the man that he is to love his wife as Christ loved the church and gave his life for her. I often hear men talk of the woman submitting but how did Christ love the Church? I do believe that the Lord's disciples were also concerned about who would be the leader amongst them, who would sit on his right or his left, but Jesus said that the greatest among you would be the greatest servant. He didn't only say this, but he took off his princely robe and washed their feet to show by example his humility and his servant nature. He reminded them that if you call me Lord and I've bowed down to wash your feet, then how much more should you do that for one another? Husbands and wives need one another in love and there's no way around that.

The Bible says in 1 Corinthians 13:13,

> 13 "And now these three remain: faith, hope, and love. But the greatest of these is love."

Love is the greatest because there will be a time when we won't need faith or hope anymore. When Jesus returns for us we won't need faith or hope because He will be with us, providing all that we need, we will always need love though. To me, this is the reason I'm more focused on love than rulership or even leadership. When we die and go before the judgement seat of Christ, I'm quite sure He's not going to care about who was in charge. The greater weight will be put on how much love we've shown throughout our lives as believers. If you loved your wife as Christ loved the church, but she refused to submit, then you will receive a reward.

In order to ensure that you've selected the right spouse, both men and women must try the spirit by the Spirit to see if they are of God. Many believers quote that scripture, but most don't know what that looks like in practicality. You must learn to taste his or her fruit. The problem is that fruit doesn't grow overnight and if you've ever tried watching anything grow, you can never see it. Once, I planted a seed and tried every day to watch it grow, but to know avail. The plant always seemed to sprout up when I wasn't looking. This is how fruit grows, if you get impatient, you will miss the chance to taste the fruit.

Far too many men choose their wife based on her looks as we are visual creatures, I get it. However, this can be disastrous if we don't examine her fruit first. I have a belief that all things can and will be revealed in time. I like to say a minimum of one year should be taken before entering into a marriage. Suppose you meet someone in the springtime of their life and you decide to marry them that very summer. Everything seems fine until autumn comes and you start to see the leaves "fall" from the bloom. Now, they are humdrum and dull when you thought that you were getting something totally different. The winter of their life could be even worse.

Our Pre-Marriage counselor had to tell us that we were done, as we had more sessions than anyone he's ever counseled. We couldn't afford to get it wrong as too much was on the line. Many couples simply don't take the time to get to know one another before marriage. One day while courting my now wife, she turned to me without warning and asked me the following question, "Drew, why do you love me so much?" Without hesitation, I replied, "You represent God to me and you are the only woman that makes me want to be a better man." I still feel the same way after twelve years of marriage. This woman is truly a gift from God and I know beyond a shadow of a doubt. My love for her is deeper and stronger than in the beginning.

Examine carefully the one you intend to marry. Let your measuring tool be the Fruit of the Spirit. Finally, they may not have all the fruit but they must have some. Over time there will be many chances to produce more Spiritual fruit and being in a committed marriage is a fertile ground to produce more fruit.

❤ ❤ ❤

Andrew and Desiree are an ordained husband and wife team. Join us for inspiring events, couple accountability, and thriving community!

Contact them at lovingthelees2012@gmail.com.

For small businesses looking for support or entrepreneurs desiring for their dreams to become a reality reach out to Andrew at andrewlee@relylocal.com.

From core to confidence, Desiree can help you get there. For more information email: desiree@bodyecelebration.com website: www.bodyecelebration.com IG: @bodyecelebrationllc

Philip & Justine Dix

Co-Hosts

THE WINNING MARRIAGES PODCAST

Phil & Justine Dix, reunited middle/high school sweethearts, now back together in the best part of their life and have been married for over six years, in September 2018. God has blessed them with the opportunity to have three beautiful, blessed, and wonderful children.

Their relationship has been reignited and they entered into marriage with Jesus Christ being the bonding agent that has not and will not break His commitment to them, as they commit themselves daily. Marriage is a passion for them because of how pivotal they know their marriage is and the inherent calling it imparts on not only the spouses, but their entire family.

Together they are branches of the ministry team for *Treasures of the Heart Worship Center* and co-hosts of *The Winning Marriages Podcast.* They love to laugh and use their individual personalities and giftings to glorify the Lord and continue to build up His Kingdom.

Built on Love

by Philip and Justine Dix

When most people think of a foundation they think of the important and permanent thing that allows building to take place. The foundation of a marriage is no different. The materials we use to form the foundation matters, based on the location and situation we find ourselves. If we look at the foundation of our actual houses we would find the base-supports, our pumps, air-conditioning, and all the inner workings of what connects us to the community around us in our pipelines.

When we carefully consider the soil type that we seek to build our base, the Bible refers to good soil as a person who is receptive and open to hearing and understanding God's word. It is essential to actively listen and embrace the message allowing it to take root to produce good fruit and positive change in our lives. God's word is the seed and our heart is the soil. Without a softened and tilled heart, we are unable to bear the fruit. We would find this in the baseline of fellowship that separates the muddy clay of human interaction from our spiritually-reinforced concrete marriage commitment.

It is imperative to ensure we are not too shallow, set on uneven ground, susceptible to flooding, or lacking in reinforcement, and without good counsel. If we are to have good soil, deep enough, strong enough, and weatherproof we must seek God as our structural engineer who tells us it is good.

Faith and fellowship are the process of finishing the work to withstand the settling weight of responsibilities and stressors that try to penetrate. It's easy to forget this groundwork beneath the life we build together. Our jobs and families require a great deal of effort and attention that may cause us to neglect the foundation. It's often only remembered when the ground is shaken beneath us or we seek shelter from the storms of life.

Without regular marriage maintenance, we wouldn't notice cracks in our foundation or recognize the spillover from the world that can cause damage. Sometimes beneath the veneer that we add to bring satisfaction, we don't even notice that a problem exists. The strength and fortitude of an unbreakable marriage union lies in the spiritual connectedness of a husband and wife.

Genesis 2:24 says,

> [24]"A man leaves his father and mother and is united to his wife, and they become one flesh." This concept is not just for cute couples-name mashups and the action of physical intimacy. There is a physical and spiritual joining that takes place.

In Ephesians 5:28-29 this is reflected again saying,

> [28]"In this same way, husbands ought to love their wives as their own bodies. He who loves his wife loves himself. [29]After all, no one ever hated their own body, but they feed and care for their body, just as Christ does the church."

There is also a direct correlation to the fact that couples share a home and have built it together. A husband and wife raise their children together. In all that we do, from the point of our marriage commitment onward, it is God's design for it to be done together. We are of one flesh under one roof under one God redeemed by one savior. We are meant to become one in so many facets that becoming one flesh through marriage seems like the simplest part of the arrangement.

Jesus also reminds us of this foundational commitment in the way that he addresses divorce,

> 6 "So they are no longer two, but one flesh. Therefore what God has joined together, let no one separate." (Matthew 19:6)

God has shown from the beginning until the end that the physical state of things was never meant to be what defines our existence. The basis of a marriage then shouldn't be built upon something so temporary either.

We often desire for our spouse to be faithful in the commitment made to forsake all others and cleave unto one another. The design of even being faithful comes from the blueprint outlined in faith. Faith according to the Oxford Dictionary *is complete trust or confidence in someone or something*. The faith we have in Jesus gives way for us to love and trust our spouse in an imperfect reflection of His example.

The way that we have allowed this idea to influence our marriage is by making Jesus a third equal part. This inclusive commitment is a decision made and honored by faith. The idea of including Jesus in our marriage places Him into an equal stead of foundation and relationship. The reason for some decisions made by a husband and some decisions made by a wife are also factored through the lenses of how Jesus would feel about the decisions. So with Jesus involved in the decision-making processes of our relationship, divorce is not an option because we know it's not a decision pleasing to Him. What God joins can't be separated because if we are joined together in a Holy matrimony then it should make the two people involved, *Holy.*

The apostle Paul refers to this same principle of Jesus in our marriage with us and how it strengthens and changes us in Ecclesiastes 4:12. The apostle Paul says,

> [12]"Though one may be overpowered, two can defend themselves. A cord of three strands is not quickly broken."

In our marriage, we can't just simply say Jesus is involved as a part of our decisions and not communicate with Him. The key to keeping a marriage on its feet is most humbly done by the husband and wife spending time on their knees in prayer for one another. Not in the way of praying for God to make right our childish and inattentive husband or to make perfect our stressful and discontented wife. Prayer and spiritual connectedness preserve not just the relationship between husband and wife but it keeps communication open with an unbiased advocate for our marriage. We need that advocate to hold fast to our love and capacity to love outside the linear and binary ways of the flesh. The advocacy of God at the beginning of our marriage is pivotal to surviving the baby stages and parenting challenges. The love and compassion for each other is a daily choice that keeps us interested in the idea of us as we survive the challenging times.

Choosing to love each other in the way the Apostle Paul calls us to love in Ephesians 5:25-27,

> [25]"Husbands, love your wives, just as Christ loved the church and gave himself up for her [26] to make her holy, cleansing her by the washing with water through the word, [27] and to present her to himself

> as a radiant church, without stain or wrinkle or any other blemish, but holy and blameless."

Marriage is not just a daily choice it's continuously choosing to love, honor, and respect the other person above ourselves. We both had lives before each other. When you choose to get married you are choosing unity; choosing to become one. It doesn't happen instantly but the vow is an oath to say I choose to learn, I choose to change, I choose to understand you, I choose to love even when, and I choose to build this new life now with you. It was easier to leave an old life behind when we chose to die to it.

Before we entered a covenant with each other, we both fell to our knees, and took a surrendering posture to God. We had to give up a life we once knew and grew so comfortable operating in, to establish a relationship with Him. We took our first steps as a couple when we dedicated ourselves to premarital counseling with our Pastors and became a witness to each other's baptism. This set the tone for the direction of our marriage. As we came up from the water, we were both born again, leaving our old lives behind, ready to grow closer to Christ together. Were there still communication issues? Yes. Were there still generational curses that needed to be dealt with? Yes. Was there still trauma from past relationships? Yes. Were there still habits gripping us from our potential in Christ? Yes. Was there a burning to grow closer to Him together? Absolutely yes and we were going to get there one day at a time with some key foundational principles. Those principles include; the triangular marriage structure with God, having a forever mindset, staying committed to marriage, dedication to ministry, and preserving the family structure.

The marriage triangle consists of three parts. At the top is God and both of us hold our connection to Him. This is not intended or suggested that we hold our connections separately because we are designed to be of one accord. The beautiful thing about being two parts of the same marriage is also the tricky part that requires us to meet our differences in the middle at the heart of God. So it might be easy to conclude that, yes, the movable two points at the bottom are us and our commitment holds us together. If we stay together and stay focused on God then we have a marriage structure that will last indefinitely. At any point in time, the marriage can stand as long as all three connections remain intact. The closer we grow to God together then the closer we get to one another. It creates a perfect relationship growth model that we can use to assess our team and become stronger.

The triangle is the perfect model because there are three parts. God himself is three parts; Father, Son, and Holy Spirit. Time is also three parts; Past, Present, and Future. We as humans are also characterized by three main parts: our mind, body, and spirit. Triangles are also the simplest existing shapes with defined points. The symbolism of the number three can be found numerous times in scripture. Triangles also represent balance and stability. When positioned on its base, a triangle represents *grounding*. Taking all the symbolism into consideration and seeking to know who God is, made this declaration more resounding to create this triangular marriage structure.

We adopted a *forever* mindset which has now been engrained and engraved into our marriage foundation. The *forever* mindset is how we can choose our marriage commitment every second of every day. We ask questions of ourselves and sometimes our spouse. The first question, "How important will this detail or discrepancy be in the grand scheme of *forever*?" If there is ever something that leads to an answer greater in gravity than "it won't" then we will talk through or break down the importance it has. The next question, "How will this detail or decision point me in the direction of Jesus and *forever*?" If the answer to the second question is "it won't" then prayer and communication need to take place before proceeding any further.

We make numerous decisions that either bring us closer to the world or closer to Christ. A husband must submit to the will of the Lord in all things. The will of God is to make each other our topmost priority only second to Himself. Even our children don't take priority over the physical and spiritual wellness of our spouse. God has proven to be trustworthy enough to take care of everything else if we submit to His will and make decisions based on His promises. Anything immersed in sin or the world is only a distraction from this divine purpose. Sin is the ultimate roadblock to us walking with Jesus into a *forever* relationship with God, our spouse, and our children.

The submission to Christ by a husband should be followed by the submission of the wife to her husband. The goal isn't to use force but to knowingly make ourselves Holy. Stopping and asking those questions seems unrealistic sometimes but it's unfair to our spouse not to try and be the best version of ourselves. Life is confusing and gets difficult at times but trying our best to equip ourselves for the *forever journey* together gets more and more realistic that we can and are doing this.

If we mirror Christ, keeping in mind the vision of *forever* and the will of God, then we have the highest chance of success in our marriage. We need to operate with an 'iron sharpens iron' mentality sprinkled with some grace, love, and understanding. The thing that still gets lost in our relationship is that while we are both focused on the same goal we have to work together. We don't want to spend so much time focused on *forever* that we forget the importance that much of the present moments have.

The practical application would be to know our words have

power, to stand by our commitment "for better or for worse", and have a forgiving heart willing to walk towards healing. Our words have life-changing impacts, they can influence others, they can bring honor or dishonor, and have the power to heal or destroy.

There are several books and umpteen scriptures in the Bible that share this wisdom with us in both encouragement and warnings. Ephesians 4:29 was impactful for us when applying a *forever* mindset. It reads,

> 29"Do not let any unwholesome talk come out of your mouths, but only what is helpful for building others up according to their needs, that it may benefit those who listen."

We want to be mindful to approach arguments and confrontations with ears to hear and a problem-solving mentality. We want to speak life into our spouse and our marriage as a whole. When we affirm each other and aspects of our marriage are going well, we force the enemy out of our business and stand on the fact that we aren't going down, we are building and growing! This IS a *forever* stance. This is saying we will not speak death upon our marriage.

Our thoughts do not have to match what we say because when we speak our brain shifts. We may think, "Life would be easier if we got a divorce or I do not want to deal with this long term," but as we speak life and ask questions such as, "How can we grow from this?" or better yet, forget the questions and go to God to pray for your spouse and the marriage, in general. Those thoughts will soon shift as your tongue speaks truth and life into the matter. There is no room for destruction when your words and heart are set on building and healing. It's a choice. This brings us to James chapter 3 in its entirety which focuses on taming the tongue:

1 “Not many of you should become teachers, my
fellow believers, because you know that we who
teach will be judged more strictly. 2 We all stumble
in many ways. Anyone who is never at fault in what
they say is perfect, able to keep their whole body in
check. 3 When we put bits into the mouths of horses
to make them obey us, we can turn the whole
animal. 4 Or take ships as an example. Although
they are so large and are driven by strong winds,
they are steered by a very small rudder wherever
the pilot wants to go. 5 Likewise, the tongue is a
small part of the body, but it makes great boasts.
Consider what a great forest is set on fire by a small
spark. 6 The tongue also is a fire, a world of evil
among the parts of the body. It corrupts the whole
body, sets the whole course of one’s life on fire, and
is itself set on fire by hell. 7 All kinds of animals,
birds, reptiles and sea creatures are being tamed
and have been tamed by mankind, 8 but no human
being can tame the tongue. It is a restless evil,
full of deadly poison. 9 With the tongue we praise
our Lord and Father, and with it we curse human
beings, who have been made in God’s likeness. 10
Out of the same mouth come praise and cursing.
My brothers and sisters, this should not be. 11 Can
both fresh water and salt water flow from the same
spring? 12 My brothers and sisters, can a fig tree
bear olives, or a grapevine bear figs? Neither can a
salt spring produce fresh water.”

We have the choice to choose words that build as mentioned in Ephesians 4, or choose words that can inflict catastrophic damage as mentioned in James 3. One leads to a life of *forever*, and the other leads to death and disappointment. We get this wrong at times. We all stumble in many ways. Unfortunately, anger is a sin that can be hard to tame which can lead to misjudgement and impulsive decisions. The important thing is how are we using our words thereafter? Are we coming to God with a heart of repentance? Are we going to our spouse with sincere remorse? And are we making an effort to improve?

There are a few things invoked by the flesh which hold the potential to cause permanent damage. Some of these things Jesus addresses in Matthew 5 when He teaches about murder/anger, adultery, divorce, and oaths. The act of anger is the loudest opponent to a relationship reflecting the Lord and a lasting *forever.* Anger in a relationship is one of the most dangerous because we invite anger into our lives. How many times have we tried to see how long we can last before anger gets the better of our day? If adultery was as gravitational and alluring as anger would marriage even be possible? In Matthew 5:21, Jesus addresses murder and in 22-24 he reminds us why we should all be slow to our approach of anger,

> 22"But I tell you that anyone who is angry with a brother or sister will be subject to judgment. Again, anyone who says to a brother or sister, 'Raca,' is answerable to the court. And anyone who says, 'You fool!' will be in danger of the fire of hell. 23"Therefore, if you are offering your gift at the altar and they remember that your brother or sister has something against you, 24 leave your gift there

> in front of the altar. First go and be reconciled to them; then come and offer your gift."

We can't truly hold our heads high in righteous anger against our spouse because we would be effectively taking anger to inflict damage on ourselves. Unbridled anger for a minute is enough to ruin the rest of someone's day or longer. When we look at adultery and divorce they are also temporary and momentary choices that sacrifice eternity. Jesus states this warning about adultery and illustrates it twice in Matthew 5:27-30,

> [27]"You have heard that it was said, 'You shall not commit adultery.' [28] But I tell you that anyone who looks at a woman lustfully has already committed adultery with her in his heart. [29] If your right eye causes you to stumble, gouge it out and throw it away. It is better for you to lose one part of your body than for your whole body to be thrown into hell. [30] And if your right hand causes you to stumble, cut it off and throw it away. It is better for you to lose one part of your body than for your whole body to go into hell."

Jesus' illustrations in this passage are the perfect example of the *forever* mindset displaying the level of discipline and dedication required for spiritual survival. The only just cause Jesus gives for divorce is adultery because that is according to the law but gives no other excuses.

> [32] "But I tell you that anyone who divorces his wife, except for sexual immorality, makes her the

> victim of adultery, and anyone who marries a divorced woman commits adultery." (Matthew 5:32)

The oath made by a husband and wife (with only that one caveat) is honored by God forever even if the promise doesn't receive fulfillment by the people involved. Wedding vows are one of the most sacred oaths made by a person, and God doesn't take any oath made with or under His name lightly. Anyone who proceeds into Holy matrimony without this understanding is essentially posturing to permanently take the Lord's name in vain.

We started to shift even deeper into a stance of commitment as our family grew. We had been involved in our church and formed such a bond with our Pastors and congregation that we just knew it would be our home long-term. We heard God tell us these people would be our new family.

As we navigated the hardships of the Covid pandemic, we stayed very connected to our Pastors and church family through as many virtual opportunities as possible. We had just recently had our son, our careers went through radical changes, and we moved into a family member's basement awaiting the very delayed build of our new home. It was a challenging year but a year full of opportunities to connect on a deeper level with Christ. We started to confront our sins and put God first. Once we found out we'd be having another baby, we began to realize the impact a strong marriage has on a household and generations.

After finally moving into our new home with a 2-year-old and newborn baby, we started working towards creating a culture that brings glory to our Heavenly Father. We both started identifying areas of our lives that we knew were not pleasing to Him. We started working harder to align ourselves onto this narrow path with Christ. As a married couple with two small children, with a pretty incredible love story that only God could pull off, we felt led to marriage ministry.

From the perspective of a Husband who loves his wife as he follows Christ, it's my life mission to keep to the word and keep to my word. In our unique situation I discovered my wife at thirteen through a wonderful friendship and declared that she would be my wife at fourteen. My wife, who at the time was my best friend, would only agree to be my girlfriend if I promised to always be her friend no matter what.

This looked like youthful folly or puppy love but the feeling in the physical and spiritual left an imprint that couldn't be destroyed or ignored. We were no longer dating by sixteen and went through the tragic stages of a teenage breakup. Even through parting ways and maturing into young adulthood, the connection and feeling of declaration left a remnant akin to an unfulfilled commitment. We both went on very different paths directly after high school with my entering into the army reserves with hopes of finding an active duty slot for the given military occupation and her being a scholar with a determined career path. We ran into each other on a random break between classes during my second semester of trying out community college, which was her last semester before heading off to graduate classes at a larger school. This brought us back into contact with each other and reignited a friendship like an accelerated blaze. This was just a point of rediscovery followed by more years of immaturity and growth but was clearing the way for something that seemed impossible before that random meeting.

The friendship promised was present again and only God could have arranged for the precise navigation and execution that would lead to a rededication, proposal, baptisms, and marriage after traumatic events and tragic losses left us both with just one another for support. Our friendship and faith have cemented our relationship and proven in our lives to be foundational to our marriage. As a husband and father, I now fully appreciate the work God has done in my life to make our family possible. This has also been a driving factor for entering into marriage ministry with our church and starting the marriage ministry podcast "Winning Marriages" which focuses on faith based marriage.

Committing ourselves to ministry was just the beginning. It was the time we moved from lukewarm to a burning desire to walk with Christ and trust God with all aspects of our marriage. When God showed us we would be on the air and internet waves with a Podcast, we had our reservations. We had listened to a few but we didn't know anything about programs, equipment, or how to use either. We took a deep dive and this 'trust fall' has landed us here.

If we are committing ourselves to the oath made, then the follow-through is not dependent upon our happiness. Happiness in our marriage comes from the amount of love and commitment we put in. Looking at professional athletes as an example, some show up just for contract fulfillment. However, the greats that we hear about winning championships, give every moment their all and sometimes sacrifice their gains for the sake of having a successful team.

Our approach to marriage mirrors the latter. Serving our spouse and serving Christ is not always comfortable. It's a humbling process where the result is good and fulfillment pours out from it. The result is evident in how our marriage has been saved by the duty we have to the marriage ministry. There have been many times where we both have thrown up our hands and said, "God you need to deal with him/her because we can't serve You properly until You fix them!" Every time this has happened God will bring about a change in the heart of the requester and a beautiful podcast or sermon has flowed forth from the breakthrough.

Our commitment to marriage has never come under a threat that God couldn't handle and He has always made a way through, for us. Our commitment to marriage and our dedication to ministry have created a tagline that allows us to better steer the swings of challenges and maneuver through obstacles. This shared piece of our relationship with the Lord has given a string to our kite so that we can properly navigate while trusting God to keep us adrift.

The finished work of our marriage is the example that we impart to our children. If we display that we have all the answers and can do this on our own, then our children will believe they have to do the same. That is a burden too great to bear, even Jesus looked to His Heavenly Father for guidance.

We want our marriage to reflect the same willingness to try but the wisdom to know that we need that same guidance. Our family is centered around one thing, love. The God we serve is Love, and we owe the Glory of everything we do or have done to Him. This marriage, our family, and our future are all thanks to having built our foundation upon Jesus Christ.

❤ ❤ ❤

God called us on a mission to start a Marriage Ministry Podcast to share his word, shine light on testimonies, and encourage others with the TRUTH! Marriage works and we are undefeated with our eyes on Christ. Check out 'The Winning Marriages Podcast!' We are a real couple serving a real God.

https://www.winningmarriagestwc.com/
https://open.spotify.com/show/5AADoV7yXXfBMUb0wGVQe2?si=9prvaETPS8urd-9sb3Ap2Q
https://www.facebook.com/winningmarriages
https://www.instagram.com/winning_marriages

Derrick & Thelma Williams

Derrick and Thelma are originally from Detroit, Michigan and have been married for six years. They both met in the second grade, back in 1978 and were high school sweethearts, but ended the relationship, mid senior year. They had completely lost all contact with each other for twenty-five years. During the course of living their separate lives, Thelma had given birth to four beautiful children and Derrick married and divorced.

Enters the invitation to their twenty-fifth class reunion. This is where the two reconnected and decided to never lose contact again. After a four year courtship, the two married and are now residing in Maryland. Derrick shares that Thelma is "the only woman in the world that I completely trust."

Derrick and Thelma truly believe their union is definitely orchestrated by the Lord.

Maintaining Love & Connection

by Derrick and Thelma Williams

Everyone is not meant to be married, but this doesn't make a person's value decrease. God knows what is best for all of us. Our advice to anyone, seeking a spouse, is to first see if you are meant to be married, by confirming God's plan for your life. Surrender to His plan. Allow God, if you are meant to be married, to reveal your spouse.

> "He who finds a wife finds a good thing and obtains favor from the lord." (Proverbs 18:22)

Before marriage, become best earthly friends. Also, pursue building a strong trust connection. After marriage, pray harder. Continuously work on yourselves. This includes healing from childhood traumas, daddy issues, and all insecurities in between...as we have discovered, all hidden issues will eventually surface. We have also learned that some issues will only surface, within the boundary of marriage. In the midst of whatever presents itself, as a potential problem, within the marriage, examine yourself. See if you are the cause of the problem. What should you ask yourself, while identifying the problem?

Is this a simple misunderstanding?
Could I have said that with a little more kindness?
Would I even date myself, if that were the first impression?
Would I like to be on the receiving end of that treatment?

Be honest, and make the correct adjustments. We truly believe that God put couples together, to help heal each other. This will ensure that they will become whole, healthy and complete individuals.

Our story began in Highland Park, Michigan, in the Fall of 1978. My first, of three, new institutions of learning, that year, was Midland Elementary School. There was a certain young lady who had sparked my curiosity, with her quiet strength, and carefully spoken words. We were both in the same second grade class, and I had been watching her character for a few weeks. My first, very intentional, interaction with Thelma Andrews, was on a sunny morning, while waiting outside of the school's front door. She was a beautiful, well-behaved, well-dressed child, who usually spoke, only when extremely necessary. I decided to walk over to Thelma and introduce her to my older brother. My brother was only one grade above us, but to me, that was a big deal. I proudly walked over to her and said, "Hi Thelma! This is my big brother Lanze." Thelma looked at us both, and studied Lanze very carefully. She then looked at me, with her big brown innocent eyes, and said, "He's not very big!" My smile slowly left my face, as I digested the "raw and uncooked" truth that had come out of that sweet little face. I had to accept that reality...and I did.

Little did I know that honest Thelma Andrews would become

my future wife. Our foundation of truth was, unknowingly, laid that day. She told me the truth, and I was willing to listen. This is what sparked our first connection. I learned that I did love her, for her candid honesty. Even now, If I need to hear the truth about myself, she will give it to me. There have been times, when she has had to brace me for a few hard truths, but I can take it. I have only grown from the truth. Love can only grow from honest truth too. This is one of the main reasons that I fell deeply in love with her. She has always been honest.

Fast forward a few years, we ended up being high school sweethearts. As a teenage girl, I would often talk to God. One day, while sitting in class, I asked God for someone, with the same honest heart, as mine. God replied to me, with a vision of Derrick's face, and said that He made someone just for me. I didn't tell Derrick about this divine encounter, until years later, but it stayed with me, for the rest of my life. By the time we had become high school seniors, we had unfortunately broken-up. The reason why? It was a combination of my strict parents, and Derrick's feelings of rejection by them. My mother was an evangelist, and my father was a deacon. My family attended a Pentecostal church, and it seemed like we were always in church. I was not allowed to wear pants, and boys were completely out of the question. This meant that Derrick and I couldn't see each other outside of school, or go on dates. I couldn't even attend my senior prom. Neither of us ever dated anyone else in high school. After graduation, Derrick moved away to Georgia, to attend college.

In college, I was beginning to build my relationship with God. I thought about Thelma every day, for about two years. When someone touches your soul, in a profound way, it can last a lifetime. I still completely trusted her, and knew that she had only been completely honest with me. Even on that day, when she told me the truth, about my big brother. In high school, we experienced the feelings of being in love, for the first time, together. Love was so brand new to the both of us. For this reason, we always stood out to each other. Our first foundation of love had been laid, as teenagers. The two relationships that I had, after Thelma, never came close to the trust that we had for each other. I found that my love can flow freely, when it's built on a foundation of trust. I never had true trust in my relationships...not even in my first marriage. After that marriage ended, God told me that I was worshiping the marriage, and not Him. He revealed to me that I was holding out hope that true love could come to it, while He had other plans for my life. God already knew where true love for me existed.

A weak foundation makes for a weak house. A strong foundation makes for a strong house. This applies to marriage. Couples set themselves up for failure, when the foundation is built on lies. Couples set themselves up for success, when the foundation is built on God. This is why we believe that love cannot flourish, if trust is not present. If our trust is not cemented in God, as individuals, then we will never truly know what true love is.

> 8"Anyone who does not love does not know God, because God is love." (1 John 4:8)

We also believe that both spouses must have an individual relationship with God, in order for their connection to stay strong to one another. It takes more than one person to keep a marriage together. It takes both spouses working with God, to make it work. Both spouses must put Him first, in order to have a truly successful marriage. If neither, or just one spouse hasn't fallen in love, with God first, it makes for a difficult marriage.

> [3]"Can two walk together, except they agree?" (Amos 3:3)

As the years rolled by, I had given birth to four beautiful children, but had never gotten married, because of what God told me, that day, in high school. I never trusted anyone enough to marry them anyway. Our peers shared about Derrick getting married and I was honestly happy for him, but I still remembered what God had told me in high school regarding him.

> [19]"God is no mere human! He doesn't tell lies or change his mind. God always keeps his promises." (Numbers 23:19 CEV)

When I decided to rededicate my life to the Lord, I made up my mind that I was never going to date again, and made God my husband. He knew my heart, and that I was sincere. This is when God opened up the door for Derrick to come back into my life.

> [4]"Delight thyself also in the Lord; and he shall give thee the desires of thine heart. [5]Commit thy way unto the Lord; trust also in him; and he shall bring it to pass." (Psalm 37: 4-5)

By the time of our twenty-fifth-class reunion, my marriage had completely dissolved. I attended, with secret hopes of seeing Thelma again. Well... during the course of the picnic, I had mingled with many of my former classmates, until I heard a familiar voice that simply said, "Hi Derrick!" For the first time in twenty-five years, I felt that familiar spark in my soul. There she was, standing directly across from me. We gave each other those familiar, friendly smiles. As I stood there, I knew that I was looking at the only person, who had never lied to me, while she looked directly back at me, reading me like a book. As we began to talk to each other, it was, as if we were transported back into that peaceful world, of just me and her, sitting against the wall, in gym class, and having the best of conversations. We talked about certain aspects of our lives, and I was so relieved that she didn't ask me if I was still married. I purposely didn't tell her that I was newly divorced. I knew that I would have to be completely honest with her about the details of it all, and truth was always our foundation. I knew that the class picnic was not the right atmosphere for that conversation. Before she left, we exchanged phone numbers, and I asked her to call me the following evening.

When Thelma did call, I told her that I had just gotten divorced. Thelma immediately asked, "What did she do to you Derrick?""How do you know that it wasn't my fault?" I proudly asked. "Because I know you! What did she do to you Derrick?"she calmly asked again. I immediately felt peace, and the honest, softness, of the love that she had for me. It was as if she was looking directly into my soul. I must have cried for at least thirty minutes, before I could form the words, to tell her what happened. Up to this point, in my life, most women, including friends and family, had automatically taken sides with my ex-wife, without knowing any details, about the divorce. I was comforted in knowing that someone, besides God, truly knew my heart. Without knowing any details of the divorce, she still saw me, crystal clear...as she always had. She truly understood my soul...Thelma patiently waited for me, and encouraged me, while I got myself together, to tell her about the details of my failed marriage. I felt completely safe, in telling her, because the trust and friendship that we had established together, as children, had never left us. I was hurting, but I felt completely connected to her...and I knew that she was the only woman in the world that I had ever truly loved, and trusted.

Four years later, after many long distance phone calls that featured many deep conversations, and Derrick taking trips back to Detroit, for dinner dates, with me, we were married. God had fulfilled the promise that He shared with me, in high school, "I made him for you!" Through years of unsuccessful relationships, heartache, heart break, pain, sadness, betrayal, lies, deceit, and various trials and tribulations, God kept His word! No matter how long it takes, or what life events point you in the opposite direction of God's promises to you, just know that God never lies, and he will surely bring it to pass.

> 3"For the revelation awaits an appointed time; it speaks of the end and will not prove false. Though it lingers, wait for it; it will certainly come and will not delay." (Habakkuk 2:3)

God had to show me that Thelma was my wife, through His eyes. I truly knew that she was my wife, after a conversation, with God, while driving home from work. God simply asked, "If you were watching your life, as a movie, would you want you and Thelma to marry each other?" I said, "Yes! Those two are perfect for each other! They both know how to give and receive love...." I just kept talking, until I realized that I was speaking about me and Thelma, in real life. That was the moment that I knew that we were going to be married.

We both brought baggage to our marriage! All couples will. Guaranteed! Thelma only touched on the strict household environment that she grew up in. Although it was a God-fearing household, being too strict and overbearing will create internal scars and wounds that could take years to heal. On the other hand, my childhood household was quite the experience too. My parents divorced when I was four-years-old. The culprits of their divorce were infidelity, mental, and physical abuse. Much of it, I witnessed firsthand. Me and my three brothers lived with our mother, while our father had visitation rights every Sunday. Let's just say the mental, verbal, and physical abuse continued, but this time, my mother was the aggressor, towards me and my brothers. The environment was Godless, and very toxic. This would often trigger me to dream of a lifestyle of peace and love. So, we've got a toxic God fearing home, and toxic Godless fearing home, coming together, under the sacred institution of marriage. To add to the pot, I had already gotten a divorce. The good news is that God brought us together, this means that He can keep us together.

The basic part that I have in Derricks' healing process, was that I had to reassure him, that I understand and appreciate his heart. I also show Derrick that we want the same things. Starting with a nontoxic marriage, and household. Derrick is big on good communication, because he saw so many bad examples of communication, as a child. I carefully listen to his ideas, thoughts, and opinions. He is always open to my input, and values it very much. If we don't agree on something, I respectfully tell him. There is no such thing of us arguing, using abusive language, or yelling. The thought of it will automatically shut us both down. We have learned to take our disagreements to God together, then wait on His answer.

> 6"In all your ways acknowledge Him, And He shall direct your paths." (Proverbs 3:6)

This year, I started declaring the Word of God over him, before he leaves for work, in the morning. This covers and encourages him during his day. He told me that no one has ever done this for him, and he appreciates it. Also, I often tell Derrick that I love him because I feel that he needs to hear it. It heals! Especially, after I know that he has had a challenging day. In short, I've learned to always try to be that "soft place" for him to land.

The basic part that I have in Thelmas' healing process, is protector. She is naturally a very giving person. However, Thelma will sometimes overcompensate. After having so many restrictions, as a child, she never wants to put anyone through it...in any way. In the past, this has caused people to take her kindness for weakness. When I see this happening, or see her worrying, I firmly tell her, "Come back baby!" She will usually say, "I'm back!" Thelma has grown in this area...and is still progressing. She doesn't want anyone to ever feel that they are ignored, or not loved...so, she usually gave an automatic yes. This is all fine, and I encourage her to keep her beautiful heart. But I have to remind her that God has to guide her giving. I have to sometimes minister to her about telling people "No". This is easy for some people, but for others, it will take going before the Lord, for the anointing of "No" to fall, where it needs to, in the heart. Thelma has asked people to speak to me, when a favor is needed, because she is still learning. To me that is growth.

I had a conversation with God. He very vividly reminded me of what my "silly" request was, to Him, for a wife. She had to be: a virgin, have at least a bachelor's degree, speak at least six different languages, come from a "well to do" family, be a foreigner, have an athletic build, and be at least 5 '7 inches. My ex-wife had met all of my requirements. But what I failed to ask God, was for the wife that He had for me...the one who He had handpicked for me. God had reminded me of this grave error that I had made, in my request for a wife, to Him. He honored my request, in order to teach me a valuable lesson. I was completely humbled by it. I promised Him that I only wanted, who he personally designed for me.

At the time that I married Thelma, she wasn't a virgin, she didn't have any college degrees, she only spoke one language, her family wasn't wealthy, she didn't have an athletic build, she was born in America, and she is only 5'3. Thelma is the complete opposite of what I originally asked God for, in a wife. His plans for me are perfect! If you want to hear God laugh, tell Him what your plans are! I am blessed that God smiled on me, when He allowed me to meet my wife, the love of my life, when we were only seven-years-old. God sparked my attention to Thelma, through truth, He cemented our connection to each other, through trust, that was established, in high school, and engraved unconditional love, in our hearts for each other, through our commitment to Him and our marriage to each other. When problems arise, we fall back on this solid foundation that God has already established in us, as a couple.

We do believe that God ordains couples, for the purpose of ministry. Of course, God is the glue that holds the marriage together. Every other week, I teach Sunday school, online, while Thelma sits in the back, off camera, praying for me, as I teach. After some lessons, Thelma will tell me about a revelation that she personally learned. God has also used her to direct my next course of study, for the next Sunday School lesson. She is always my eyes and ears, while I minister.

In retrospect, during our dating season, we had to ask God to reveal our purpose to each other. What is His plan for bringing us together? In the process, God allowed us to see a glimpse of each other, as He sees us. Seeing ourselves through Gods' eyes gave us an added respect for each other. We were shown our divine purposes. Understanding each other's heart, purpose, strengths and weaknesses, has caused us to learn how to be patient with each other. It has also opened the door for us to learn more about certain areas of ourselves. There are some faults that God will only allow us to see, in each other, and allow only us, as a couple, to pray through, because we are the closest humans to each other. There are very deep things that only we and God know, specifically, about each other. We use this as an opportunity to strengthen our relationship with God, and each other.

God's plan is perfect and without flaw! God hand picked His couples! Part of the revelation is that married couples are each other's assignment. The assignment is to make sure that you both assist each other in completing the divine assignment that God has given you. In short, to fulfill the call and purpose in your lives...as a married couple. Both spouses' strengths and weaknesses are designed to assist in successfully completing the divine assignment. Also, there is never a reason for either spouse to raise their voice to each other, especially when the assignment is understood. For example, we already know that our intentions are always good towards everyone. We already know that we are each other's closest earthly friend. We both understand this. The foundation is solidly laid out, by God. We have trust, honesty, and love...the core fundamental components of our marriage. This was really already established, before earth existed. My first reaction to, what may be a simple misunderstanding, is to always give her the benefit of the doubt, and hear her side of things. That's right, I call this exposing the Devil! Not allowing confusion to settle in... being slow to anger, no need for me to ever raise my voice, because I see her heart through it all. In short, operating in love will cover you!

We hope and pray that our story can serve as a source of

hope to married couples, and soon to be married couples. While we were in the waiting process, for marriage, did we ever get discouraged sometimes? Why certainly yes! Therefore, we had to make it our business, to trust that everything is in divine order. Don't let yourselves get discouraged, to the point that you forget that God knows exactly what He is doing. If it takes a while for things to come full circle, just remember that God's time table is different from yours. Don't compare your life to anyone else's. God has hand tailored your life, to fit only you! Hold on to the promises that God has revealed to you. Keep negative people and things out of your life, and submit completely to God. By us both maintaining our love and connection to God, He, in turn, caused us to learn how to maintain our love and connection to each other. We have never regretted, trusting and waiting on the Lord. Trust Him completely. We dare you to do it!

❤ ❤ ❤

We invite you to attend our church, **Treasures of the Heart Worship Center**, located in the heart of Frederick, Maryland at **629 N. Market Street, Frederick, Maryland 27102**. Derrick is a minister serving at the church and oversees the Sunday School Ministry. We are a welcoming, creative, and vibrant place to experience God's love. Our motto is, **"Real People, Serving a Real God."** Worship, praise, and flowing in God's Word are at the heart of our services. To learn more about our church, visit **www.TreasuresWC.com** and **river4me10@gmail.com.**

Jermaine & Brittani Williams

Entrepreneurs

CYBERGUIDE IT SERVICES INC & RNR XSCAPES

The Williams couple has reached an impressive milestone of 18 years of marriage, exemplifying a remarkable blend of cultural richness and professional excellence. Jermaine is from Jamaica and Brittani hailing from South Carolina, bringing a deep sense of cultural heritage to their family. They are the parents to four children spanning pre-K to college age.

Brittani, a Southern Bell, is a devoted and dedicated wife and mother. She is a Certified Makeup Artist, Travel Agent, and an entrepreneur with successful businesses; RnR Xscapes and B. Nicora Makeup Artistry. Her nurturing spirit is complemented by her extensive IT and Program/Project Management (PM) experience. She holds a Bachelors in Telecommunication Management and Masters in Project Management. Her commitment to development is evident through her involvement with Zeta Phi Beta Sorority, Inc.

Jermaine is a devoted husband and father who wholeheartedly embraces the wisdom and values passed down by the strong men in his family. He shares Brittani's dedication to community services through his company CyberGuider IT Services Inc., inspiring youth through tech exposure after over two decades in IT. He has a Bachelors in Technical Management and holds various Cyber Security certifications.

They synergize their professional and philanthropic efforts, creating a legacy of empowerment and unity. Their partnership embodies mutual respect and a shared vision for fostering growth and excellence in all they undertake. Together, they serve as a testament to the strength and harmony achieved through complementary backgrounds and shared values.

Foundation Is Key

by Jermaine and Brittani Williams

A strong foundation in marriage is not merely the cornerstone of love and commitment but the shared understanding that enduring journeys are built on resilience, empathy, and an unshakable belief in one another's humanity. We were profoundly blessed to have found this in each other that transcends our union and family. We found this in our early twenties. Some might say that's way too young but we did and all because we set the foundation for dating and marriage.

By the time, we were an official couple in 2003, we established non-negotiables based on past relationships and experiences that neither of us were eager to relive. It was important to establish a set of foundational goals that helped us navigate our dating life which would later cultivate into the fabric that laid the foundation for our spiritual, married, and family life.

When we were dating, we understood each other's viewpoint on God and family as we were both Christians and raised in church; Brittani being Baptist and Jermaine being Seventh Day Adventist (SDA). We also cherished our vision of family. Jermaine's family, who are Jamaican, is closer knit while Brittani's family is loosely knit, so that was something she yearned for and respected within Jermaine's family. Friendships that were established before the relationship remained intact regardless of their gender unless he/she threatened our relationship. Of course, we did not expect each other to ditch our best friends however, new friends should be known to both. There were no surprise/hidden friends out of a matter of respect. With that being said

Foundational Goal #1:
~God, Family then Friends ...in that order! ~

Another aspect that was important to us was being respectful of one another, ensuring each got the treatment and love they deserved and commanding that early. You cannot allow disrespect or bad behavior for years and then expect someone to change within an instant. That has to be nipped in the bud early. We also firmly believed that your word was your BOND, dishonesty will not be tolerated! By showing compassion and respect, we would be thoughtful in the things we said and done to not put one another into a disrespectful position. For example; We will not hang up on the other while the other is still talking; If a heated discussion is had, do not walk away while the other is talking; or do not talk to the other crazy/rude/disrespectfully in our home or in front of our friends and family. Basically, don't push each other to wrath nor go to bed angry as we know tomorrow is not promised. This describes our

Foundational Goal #2:
~ Be Respectful, Kind, and Honest~

Family and individual development is super important to both of us and are key factors in our marital success. We always understood that what we build is a launching pad for our kids to excel, beyond us. We always have a growth mindset of moving in an upward trajectory, along with the belief that all who join our family should also want more for themselves. For example; a husband finds value in his wife and vice versa. This value can be attributed to a wife taking care of herself (medically, spiritually, physically, etc.), investing in a hobby, or the way she leads the family. No one should drive a wedge in the core of the family either but also, we protect our extended family and care for them as well. We have a very diverse household that embodies multi-cultural and multi-generation relationships. Jermaine's parents and Brittani's dad reside within the home. Our home comprises ages 2 to 70 years of age. We work as a unit to help each other foster good and healthy relationships. However, it's easy for people to pass their place (boundaries) as our Caribbean parents would say which leads to

Foundational Goal #3:
~Set proper expectation and boundaries
with friends and family up front~

Let's backtrack a little to when we met and started working on and implementing these goals. In the fall of 2003 Brittani and I met at work. Brittani was a Project Coordinator and I was a Technician that supported the east coast. Neither of us had ever talked or seen each other in the office but both knew and heard of each other. I would go to Sherrie's office, like three times a week, to receive my next assigned job. I noticed this young lady (Brittani) always sitting in her office when I swung by. See Sherrie was like the "IT-Rex" at the job and knew all things lab and IT so when Brittani ran into unique issues, Sherrie would help her troubleshoot them. One day I popped my head in for assistance with Sherrie, got straight to the point of what was needed and I was out of there. No words were shared between me and Brittani but a casual smile to say,"I see YOU, young lady" .

At the time of our exchange I did not know her name but I soon learned, from the team, her name was Brittani. Every guy in the office was talking about her and her beauty. I kept my distance because I believed that she would be bombarded with suitors. Because of this belief, I put her out of my mind.

A few weeks later, me and the team were having lunch, and like all lunches with the guys, we were talking about the upcoming 7v7 football (i.e., soccer) league. This year in particular the league was only offering co-ed teams so we needed two females to play and they were short one lady. One of the guys said, "I heard the new girl, Brittani, plays soccer. Jermaine, you should ask her to join the team." I said, "I'm not the Captain so whosoever that is should ask not me." I further stated that based on how she carried herself, Brittani seemed too fancy for the sport. The guys decided at that moment that I was the Captain of the team and recruitment was now my job. I conceded, "Fine, but look how the answer will be NO!" My friend Kwesi laughed as if he knew something I did not.

To my surprise, Brittani said "YES" to joining the team after sharing that she played in high school for four years. I still wrestled with the thought and my pre-assumed assessment of her potential soccer skills and abilities, but I went with it. Brittani told me that she wore the number #10, from what I knew of the sport, that is a number reserved for good players on the team. I thought, "Maybe she used to be good when her fanciness wasn't a thing" but the team needed a player and the team was depending on me to secure the last female to play, so I did. This was the most I had spoken to Brittani or anyone at the office for that matter. Another surprising response was when I asked her for her number so she could be added to the team roster for future communications. I asked her if there was a particular time I could call to inform her about practice, as I wanted to be respectful to her situation. Brittani responded confidently, "Call me anytime, this is my phone and I pay the bill!"

With the team now secure, we met up for a practice and kicked around the ball. After about an hour we noticed it was just us two there. I apologized for our team's lack of showing up to practice and assured her that she was not wasting her time. After a couple more passes and defensive plays, we both felt a connection beyond the game but quickly denied our feelings.

Practices came and went, and at this point, we shared a few more words in the office. I realized that Brittani was just a dolled-up tomboy and I liked it. She became one of the fellas clowning and holding her own on the video games, whooping our butts at times.

Insert Sherrie, seeing the potential sparks between us, she thought she would play matchmaker and sign us up to make a potluck dish together for the annual holiday office party. I (Brittani) loved to cook and showcase my talents. Jermaine was not familiar with this tradition, but was requested to prepare one of his native (Jamaican) dishes. I was excited to work on this dish, but had no idea what was in store for me that evening. We ran into some challenges with the dish and Jermaine thought it was best to call his mother, back in Jamaica, for an assist. This led to a grocery store run and me being on the phone with his mom. That was quite the disaster as I could not understand his mom's thick Patois (their native language) and his mom had no idea what I was saying. Somehow, we got through the conversation to secure the items that were needed to take corrective action.

As time passed we continued our friendship but grew closer

when we got the news that our close coworker and friend, Sherrie, had passed away after being out on extended medical leave. We attended her repass together and from that point forward there was a deeper understanding that everyone and everything has a purpose. It was evident to us that her purpose in our life was to bring us together. We proceeded to date, but that brought forth new obstacles and challenges that definitely tested our fate and relationship.

I recall when I visited Jermaine's townhouse, he had a true bachelor's pad. Not much furniture or food in the home and I guess this was by design because he was never home. The only challenge with that was, in complexes when the exterminator sprays one apartment the bugs flee to the next and Jermaine's apartment was no exception. These little unwanted friends were everywhere, the microwave, fridge, cabinets all unbeknownst to Jermaine, when I came over to his home for the first time. It was basically "Joe's Apartment" up in there, like the movie. Now I was no stranger to these pests as I did not grow up in an affluent home or neighborhood. I addressed it accordingly on our first date but Jermaine was clearly embarrassed by this discovery, nevertheless.

Jermaine had plans for dinner and a movie but I had different plans. I showed up with six cans of Raid® bug fogger, trash bags, gloves, and an old vacuum cleaner. Jermaine asked, "What is all this for?" I responded, "Our date." Jermaine was puzzled and scratching his head and decided to go along with the plan as I put all the dishes and food/pantry items into the trash bags. I walked around the house and proceeded to put three cans of fogger downstairs and three upstairs and proceeded to set them off. We rushed out the door to avoid the toxic fumes. Jermaine, being unfamiliar with this process said "What's next?" I said, "Dinner and a movie."

When we returned back, the dining room floor was covered with bugs as if they were trying to escape to freedom but could not make it to the exit. We cleaned together; I opened the windows, pulled out the vacuum, and took care of the corpses while Jermaine wiped the place down. Jermaine kept himself neat and clean so this was not a reflection of who he was! Also, he lived out of a suitcase and did not have anything but a bed, a computer desk and a weight bench in the home. No judgement here Jermaine, I have your back! Once complete, I said jokingly, "Cleanliness is next to godliness and if we are going to be together there is no place for them and us."

Proverbs 31:27 says

> 27 She looketh well to the ways of her household,
> and eateth not the bread of idleness.

We were not married but Brittani was operating as a virtuous woman, setting expectations on how she lived and would manage her household, if our relationship grew. There were numerous times when Brittani demonstrated a high level of unselfish giving and hustle. This gave Jermaine the chance to preview what life would be like if they were ever in need. It was also known that there was no interest in "playing house" for four years. Brittani's exact words were, "Don't let the fifth year catch you and we are not married." Jermaine took this as an ultimatum although Brittani was just setting the expectations up front. She was looking for something that was lasting and real and hoped Jermaine was looking for the same. As Jermaine tells the story of their union, Brittani found out that this was one of many pivotal moments that made Jermaine feel she was the one.

As our relationship blossomed and we were in the midst of

planning a wedding, welcoming our first child (Jaiden), and purchasing our first home, we were rocked by a shocking discovery regarding Brittani's past relationship—the ultimate betrayal by a friend. Brittani was devastated by the news and I watched helplessly as Brittani went through all the emotions. At this moment I knew that I had to protect my family by any means necessary. Instead of joining in the anger, with Brittani, towards her friend, I chose to go a different route. I remembered a small traveling Bible given by my mom the day I left my home country of Jamaica. In it, my parents stated "He is not far, and whenever you don't have or can't find the answer trust in the scriptures."

I spent some time finding scripture to encourage Brittani in this difficult time such as Proverbs 17:9 which says

> "Whoever would foster love covers over an offense, but whoever repeats the matter separates close friends."

As well as Colossians 3:13 which states

> "Bear with each other and forgive one another if any of you has a grievance against someone. Forgive as the Lord forgave you."

I also prayed with her to find peace throughout the situation. During this time, it was hard for me to watch the love of my life go through this betrayal without being able to help.

Not sure if you didn't realize this by now, but I am a fix-it kind of guy, if you don't want it fixed, please don't tell me. I woke up many nights during this time hearing Brittani praying for God to release the feelings she had because of the betrayal. She asked for the strength to focus on her life with me and the blessings in her belly. Again, I only encouraged and didn't take it personally. I knew she needed space to process so she could move on. I chose to be a sounding board and kept pointing her to scriptures because I didn't have the answer. I later found out that this was the moment Brittani chose me as her person for life. I truly have been happy ever since. She expressed that she did not choose me solely for how I made her feel but because of my unconditional love towards her. This was the first test of honesty, kindness and respect in our relationship but surely not the last.

The next example of these types of tests was when we were in the process of purchasing our first home and planning our wedding. With these two major decisions, as a young couple, everyone wanted to weigh in, friends and family alike. But God's presence was far greater! We got a call from Wreneisha, our Realtor, while at church, to tell us about a home for sale. We left the church and went directly to look at the house. We never heard or thought of the neighborhood she brought us to. We loved the house but there was one problem, they needed a check deposit to hold the property and secure our home from other potential buyers. We had no checks so Brittani and I were feeling dismayed as we might not find another home like that one. But God! Brittani went to the car to get something and picked up her Bible and we kid you not our bank starter checks fell out in front of us. Talk about God's blessings! We put down $500 earnest money that day to walk into the next chapter of our lives. With this home, we were able to grow our family not in the way you may think but with our extended family.

We both decided that we wanted to enter into marriage with an ironclad foundation and worked with our pastor, K. Boswell at New Hope SDA Church, to seek marriage counseling. Marriage counseling was instrumental in our success as a couple because we were both coming from different worlds, literally, with different upbringings and expectations. Brittani was a military brat and had a different outlook on life and had unique experiences and Jermaine had a different worldly view of things as well as unique experiences that required mutual acclimation. Our varied upbringing and differing cultures presented themselves within our sessions with Pastor Boswell. Pastor helped us discuss a mirage of topics (i.e culture, communication, trust, boundaries, etc.) and navigate these uncharted waters in our relationship. We had to arrive at the point where we identified the aspects of being equally yoked and all that was needed to get up to the altar. We chose to get married on 07/07/07 as it represented completion, in the Bible, and there was only one church that had that date available, Woosley Baptist Church. This church had its own requirements for counseling as well so not only did we go through weeks of it with our Adventist pastor but we went through a few more with the pastor at the Baptist church. One cool and unique thing about our wedding was that we had the fortune of having our wedding officiated by an Adventist and Baptist pastor which we felt was the perfect bridging of our union.

Picture this, a newly married couple with a new home, new baby, along with our multicultural parents and multi-generational family members all living under one roof. We will wait for that to sink in. We know we took on the impossible but God knew we could handle it and what was in store for us. We learned early that firm boundaries had to be set and maintained. This included but was not limited to establishing that all decisions stopped with us, as husband and wife. We would consider all input solicited or not but the ultimate decision was ours. Parenting style and the direction of our family was another area that we stood firm on. We knew that there's great value in learning from our elders, but also knew that we needed to develop our own parenting style and develop the foundation and principles for our family. If we just did what everyone told us to do, we would have been drones and not evolved. We decided to take the generational and cultural knowledge we had and expound upon that to raise our "Jamerican" kids. Our kids experience us firsthand as their caregivers and they also are present in the daily care of our parents, our elders. It's as if our children are living with walking history and raised by the village as their grandparents always have a story to tell or a lesson to teach. We know you are probably getting tired of hearing this, but we were BLESSED for our multi-generational and multicultural household.

This was not without heartburn here and there. Lines were being stepped on and we did have to inform the grandparents that they were here as a supportive role when needed, but most importantly to enjoy their grandchildren. We discussed how matters would be addressed in the home and then requested our first family meeting to identify baseline exceptions. This meeting did not go off perfectly but boundaries were set and discussions were had about non-negotiated areas as everyone was learning how to coexist in the same space. It took for all parties to believe in the vision and goal of the family and redefine what IN-LAWS meant in our family. We made the decision that we will not exist as IN-LAWS but just daughter and son. It took us some time to get it right and harmony was achieved by allowing anyone, young or old, to call a family meeting to discuss items of concern.

We handle situations by never picking a side but merely having a discussion with all parties involved to hear their concerns. If a family member is wrong, we try to understand why they felt, thought, or believed in their truth and then communicate observations of the situation. Surprisingly, when challenges are addressed in this manner, we usually find a resolution and reduce recurrence. It was also important to not focus on the person when a problem arose but the behavior or action of the person and how that made the other party feel. This helped de-escalate situations and really helped foster healthy discussions and conflict resolution. While these family conversations ended in a positive result, there were numerous matters we just had to take to God in prayer.

As we fast forward to today, four beautiful kids later (Jaiden, Jasmin, Brielle and Bryson), the foundational goals that we established as girlfriend and boyfriend continue to develop and solidify our marriage. It truly has been easier said than done. All of these items were tested over the years and still to this day. Over time we have mastered how to communicate within our family and more importantly, with each other. We accepted non-destructive behaviors and helped each other grow. We were purposeful and patient in all our actions and decisions. We also do annual assessments (i.e goals, priorities, aspirations, etc) as a fun activity on our anniversary and reflect on the results from time to time. Sometimes we are on track, with our goals, and sometimes we have pivoted to ensure alignment.

It's interesting to reflect on where our point of view and marital mindsets were in the beginning, in 2007, to where we are now building upon our strong foundation. We understand that marriage is a work in progress and if you don't stick to the foundation, things can easily go off the rails or crumble. With God being the cornerstone of our marriage, we fully devote everything to building a strong and healthy relationship with each other and our family which is key to a solid foundation. We challenge you to take an assessment of your marital foundation, and develop marital goals for the next 3-5 years. Re- evaluate the assessment annually and see how you've evolved as a couple. Ask yourselves, have your results changed? If so, how? What was the change? Does it make your foundation stronger and can you improve upon anything?

❤ ❤ ❤

Jermaine is the Founder/CEO of **CyberGuider IT Services Inc.** and Brittani is CyberGuiders' Scholarship and Community Service Director. If your organization needs assistance to meet Information Technology (IT) security requirements, seek compliance consultants, and services on how to protect your data from cyber-attacks contact **CyberGuider IT Services Inc**. at info@cyberguider.com or https://cyberguider.com.

In addition, Brittani is an entrepreneur with an Independent Travel Agency, **RnR Xscapes.** If you are looking for experiences tailored to your dreams with unparalleled elegance and impeccable service let **RnR Xscapes** curate your next adventure. Contact them at rnrxscapes@gmail.com.

Wisdom in Love

Advice from Couples

Marriage is a journey, a tapestry woven with moments of joy, challenges, growth, and unwavering commitment. It's a partnership that requires constant nurturing, effort, and intentionality to thrive. While every marriage is unique, there are universal principles and practices that can inspire couples to continue building and strengthening their bond.

In this final chapter, we share pearls of wisdom gathered from 15 couples who graciously participated in our survey. Representing a diverse range of marital experiences—from newlyweds to those celebrating decades of togetherness—these couples offered heartfelt advice on how to keep improving and nurturing their relationships.

Through their shared stories and practical insights, you'll find reminders of what it means to work together as a team, prioritize love and respect, and keep the flame of connection burning. Whether you're just starting your marital journey or years into the commitment, these lessons serve as a testament to the resilience and beauty of love when tended with care.

Let these voices inspire you, encourage you, and remind you that a strong marriage is not about perfection but about progress—a daily choice to love, grow, and cherish one another.

Virginia Couple Married Since October 14, 2000

How did you know they were the "one" for you?

A: *When I immediately met him, I was infatuated. He was very sexy, well spoken, and welcoming. He was so kind and attentive.*

S: *Holy Spirit spoke to me saying, "There is your wife!"*

Marital Advice

A: *It is critical to recognize that you are TWO different people and it's okay to embrace yourself but marriage is about mutual submission.*

S: *Advise honesty from the beginning of the relationship. Monogamy is also important to establish and maintain throughout your marriage.*

What are some practices, nuggets of reflection, or beliefs that helped you two to navigate through the hard times?

A: *Faith in God and ensuring He's the head of our marriage.*

S: *Building our four walls and staying committed to our goals.*

Virginia Couple Married Since October 13, 2012

How did you know they were the "one" for you?

G: *In college, our relationship was stronger than most and we were together for some rough times and she never wavered or faltered.*

S: *The way he treated my special needs brother. He was kind and understanding and was always willing to help.*

Marital Advice

G: *understand what patience means and how much value it holds in a marriage.*

S: *COMMUNICATION!! If there is a problem, speak about it and don't let it fester.*

What are some practices, nuggets of reflection, or beliefs that helped you two to navigate through the hard times?

G: *God in the center and laughter.*

S: *Keeping God in center and he makes me laugh so much. I love that about him.*

♥

Maryland Couple Married Since March 15, 2019

How did you know they were the "one" for you?

E: *The way he comforted me; the way he took care of me while I was at my most vulnerable emotionally and physically without an ulterior motive was everything to me. The way he showed me out; encouraged my thoughts and feelings and always wanted to hear me. Like really hear me. (oh how things have changed lol) I met someone that wanted to know me for me and not for them or how it could benefit them. Never judging me for my past decisions, relationships and thoughts nor throwing it in my face when it could have benefited them or I may have done. I knew waaay before he did. He would be my person. This is the person I dreamed and prayed for.*

G: *We became friends first to understand some of each other's wants, needs and boundaries.*

Marital Advice

G: *Be patient with your partner!*

E: *Ask God to lead and develop a relationship with God for your relationship as a unit. God will check you way before your partner does.*

What are some practices, nuggets of reflection, or beliefs that helped you two to navigate through the hard times?

G: *God, Prayer, friendship and being intentional.*

E: *prayer and friendship*

Maryland Couple Married Since March 19, 2015

How did you know they were the "one" for you?

He was intentional in his desire to commit.

Marital Advice

Build your foundation on shared values and faith.

What are some practices, nuggets of reflection, or beliefs that helped you two to navigate through the hard times?

Try to focus on each other's effort rather than each other's faults.

Virginia Couple Married Since July 3, 2010

How did you know they were the "one" for you?

C: *I watched her in a serving capacity while volunteering and I thought, "Wow, I would love to be married to her." But when we talked on the phone for the first time and I got to know the personality, the humor, I was shook.*

J: *I had been married before and seen how badly things can go when only one person has committed to the vows. Cory was intentional to let me know during our first phone conversation what type of husband he would be. I knew then that I was in for true love.*

Marital Advice

Before marrying, discuss the parameters and nonnegotiables of acceptance of each person as they grow and change into an evolved person. Know if the soul match is enough to endure each person's evolution.

What are some practices, nuggets of reflection, or beliefs that helped you two to navigate through the hard times?

Laughter, common goals, prayer, space, coparenting, humility, and commitment to self betterment.

Virginia Couple Married Since June 22, 2019

How did you know they were the "one" for you?

E: *When I found myself praying for him when we weren't in a "good" place.*

J: *I can't explain it, it was this one time when she looked at me and it filled my heart.*

Marital Advice

Seek God first and be sure to do marriage counseling.

What are some practices, nuggets of reflection, or beliefs that helped you two to navigate through the hard times?

Learning how God created marriage and how to apply His Word to our situation.

Maryland Couple Married Since October 18, 2013

How did you know they were the "one" for you?

C: *I knew Saucey was the one because of his integrity and honest heart!*
S: *I knew Christina was the one because of her nurturing unselfish ways.*

Marital Advice

C: *I would say listen to learn and not to just have a "comeback" communicate issues and implement ways to correct things. And laugh :)*
S: *Continue to have a friendship at the root of the relationship.*

What are some practices, nuggets of reflection, or beliefs that helped you two to navigate through the hard times?

Just being open to communicate when each other needs to. We are good at that :)

North Carolina Couple Married Since January 10, 1993

How did you know they were the "one" for you?

D: *We were the only ones who could put up with the other long-term.*

K: *Seriously though, we got along. We had things in common but also realized we were our own people and supported those differences.*

Marital Advice

Pick your battles. There are many things in life that simply are not worth arguing over. Before you decide to argue, think of your words. Often what ends up as an argument is simply one not understanding the other and needing a different explanation. Watch your tone. The tone can change how your words are perceived. Understand that people trigger stack. That snap may not be directed at you but a response to a rough day and mental exhaustion. Own your emotions, recognize why you feel that way, explain, apologize. Learn from your ways and work to change.

What are some practices, nuggets of reflection, or beliefs that helped you two to navigate through the hard times?

The willingness to talk and calm down.

Ohio Couple Married Since June 10, 2017

How did you know they were the "one" for you?

Everything was so easy when we were together.

Marital Advice

Never lose sight of your spouse even when you are at odds with one another.

What are some practices, nuggets of reflection, or beliefs that helped you two to navigate through the hard times?

Our faith and relationship with Christ carries us through more than anything. Allowing us to see our mate through Christ's eyes, not ours. During hard conversations, fully listen to your spouse. Listen with intention and purpose to understand one another and learn what the other person needs.

Virginia Couple Married Since September 4, 1982

How did you know they were the "one" for you?

R: *During our dating period I knew he was a man of God, He always treated me with respect, placed his family first and loved his career.*

M: *I trusted her with my money.*

Marital Advice

R: *Keep God first in your marriage. Be there during the good days and bad days. Raise your children to become successful adults. Have disagreements, but always with respect. Never lose the spark.*

M: *Find someone with a similar family base which gives a good possibility of a successful relationship.*

What are some practices, nuggets of reflection, or beliefs that helped you two to navigate through the hard times?

R: *Prayer and working through it together.*

M: *Faith and my parents as my example.*

Virginia Couple Married Since June 9, 1997

How did you know they were the "one" for you?

Not really sure. Just felt right.

Marital Advice

Don't give up!

What are some practices, nuggets of reflection, or beliefs that helped you two to navigate through the hard times?

We made a commitment and will keep going at it!

Virginia Couple Married Since July 7, 2007

How did you know they were the "one" for you?

You have to read our chapter to find this out. - Jerome & Brittani

Marital Advice

Anything that might help someone else. I know what might work for us might not work for others. One thing we would say is command the respect you deserve and if you do not like a certain behavior or habit nip that in the bud soonest. It's hard to get people to change one behavior that has been accepted or allowed. I.e if you don't like profanity or it being used towards you express that...if you don't like a smoker...make that be known. If you don't like being talked down to or talked at then vocalize that. Secondly don't go to sleep mad or with things on your heart as tomorrow is not promised. Lastly, continue to court and date one another, especially if you have kids because one day those kids will leave and if you haven't done that there will be a disconnect. Can't lose yourself in the kids...lol.

What are some practices, nuggets of reflection, or beliefs that helped you two to navigate through the hard times?

Communication, Compassion and Commitment...along with some Counseling from time to time...there is nothing wrong with a tune up here or there. Staying connected to our spiritual journey and core values. Having mutual respect for one another while navigating change and challenges with having the end goal in mind which is overcoming this bump in the road as our union is important and will be stronger for it.

Maryland Couple Married Since July 24, 2024

How did you know they were the "one" for you?

We complemented each other.

Marital Advice

Keep God first!

What are some practices, nuggets of reflection, or beliefs that helped you two to navigate through the hard times?

Communication and Compromise

Virginia Couple Married Since October 26, 2002

How did you know they were the "one" for you?

She loved and respected me regardless of what I had and who I was.

Marital Advice

Highly suggest you live together prior to getting married and discuss items from religion(how you are raising your kids) and goals. How do you see each other in 5, 10, 30 years from now?

What are some practices, nuggets of reflection, or beliefs that helped you two to navigate through the hard times?

Nothing breaks our relationship. Through thick and thin.....live by it.

Couple Married Sincc November 12, 2016

Maryland

How did you know they were the "one" for you?

D: *I had an undeniable feeling that Sasha was the one.*

S: *David's care for how I felt and the things I expressed along with accepting my child as his own.*

Marital Advice

Do your best to gain clarity on who you are, what you need, and what you value. Ask questions about everything to understand each other's viewpoints. As well as, create an identity outside of your spouse.

What are some practices, nuggets of reflection, or beliefs that helped you two to navigate through the hard times?

Determining what we could live with that the other person wasn't or that the other person couldn't do. Accepting our differences in our communication styles and doing the work to heal on individual issues so that we weren't projecting those on each other.

HOW CAN WE BE OF SERVICE TO YOU?

Forever and a Day Publishing LLC turns writers' dreams into reality by offering personalized, faith-centered support throughout the self-publishing journey. With a foundation built on values of God, Family, Career, and Finances, we empower authors to share their unique stories and leave a lasting impression.

Turn Your Story into a Published Book with Forever and a Day Publishing!

FAAD
FOREVER AND A DAY PUBLISHING, LLC

Have you dreamed of seeing your book on the shelves, in readers' hands, or available online? Are you overwhelmed and unsure of how to write and publish a book? Do you know of someone who has shared about wanting to become an author?

At Forever and a Day Publishing, we specialize in transforming your writing dreams into reality. We've created the perfect package for your writing desires. Whether it's fiction, nonfiction, or memoirs, we are here to guide you through every step of the publishing process.

Your story matters, and the world needs to hear it! Let us help you bring it to life.

Contact us today to get started on your journey to becoming a published author!

https://faadpublishingllc.com

www.ingramcontent.com/pod-product-compliance
Lightning Source LLC
Chambersburg PA
CBHW072157100925
32435CB00011B/300
979899117O314